MODERN
EUCHARISTIC
AGREEMENT

LONDON SPCK 1973

First published in 1973
by S.P.C.K.
Holy Trinity Church
Marylebone Road
London NW1 4DU

Made and printed in Great Britain by
The Talbot Press
Saffron Walden, Essex

SBN 281 02766 8

CONTENTS

Foreword, by the Right Reverend Alan C. Clark
Joint Chairman of the Anglican-Roman Catholic
International Commission   v

Introduction: Documents on Modern Eucharistic Agreement
by the Right Reverend H. R. McAdoo
Joint Chairman of the Anglican-Roman Catholic
International Commission   1

Anglican-Roman Catholic International Commission:
An Agreed Statement on Eucharistic Doctrine   23
Windsor 1971

The Eucharist as Sacrifice:
A Lutheran-Roman Catholic Statement   33
St Louis, Missouri, 1967

Group of Les Dombes:
Towards a Common Eucharistic Faith?
translated by Pamela Gaughan   51

The Eucharist in Ecumenical Thought:
Statement of the Faith and Order Commission of the
World Council of Churches   79
Louvain 1971

FOREWORD

The publication of four important Eucharistic Agreements is an initiative of great value for the growth of the Ecumenical Movement. It responds to a widespread demand for documentation from those who are determined to further the cause of organic unity. The skilled analysis of the Bishop of Ossory in his introductory essay reveals not only the remarkable similarity in the conclusions of the groups involved in the separate dialogues, but also the emergence of a common *method*—a result which may have even greater repercussions than the consensus obtained.

All Christian traditions confess Christ as present in their eucharistic celebrations, a vivid witness itself to a fundamental belief in the resurrection. The majority regard the eucharist as the *locus* where Christ is uniquely present, and see this presence as mysteriously related to the elements of bread and wine. They also situate the Church's celebration in the context of the one and all-sufficient sacrifice of Christ our Lord whereby the world was redeemed.

But the exact meaning, and therefore the particular formulation of belief, which each tradition attributes to these relationships, is not all of a kind. What has emerged, however, in these recent years is an increasing measure of agreement as to the content of Christian faith in the eucharistic mystery. There has been no intention to disparage, let alone dismiss, the traditional formularies, but rather to identify the express purpose of our ancestors in constructing those formularies and to uncover the abiding common understanding that was untouched by apparent conflict and even contradiction. At the same time, over and above this historical approach, the parties involved in the dialogues conceived it their task to testify to their *present* eucharistic faith, particularly as to the central core of their belief, namely, the question of eucharistic presence and eucharistic sacrifice.

It will be quite evident to the student of the documents that some groups chose a far wider canvas than others. Some presented a rich conspectus of the totality of the Church's belief in this great mystery. Others, with deliberate intention, restricted themselves with theological rigour to the exact areas of disagreement and opposition. Both approaches are necessary if we are to understand our present situation. It is increasingly difficult, though in my opinion necessary, to treat subjects like eucharist and ministry in strict isolation. The feeling that doctrinal agreement must be matched by pastoral directive is also apparent in the texts that follow. Hence the scarcely veiled pressure for some solution to the vexed question of intercommunion. Whereas theological precision would argue against it, the concrete situation, some feel, would argue for a modicum of exceptional practice. At the same time no suggestion is made for any unilateral initiative without the consent of church authority.

An attentive study of these contemporary agreements as to the meaning and purpose of the eucharist, the sacrament of unity, will lift up the hearts of all who, in a spirit of courage and hope, look to the future which is embodied in the Prayer of Christ. The grace of ecumenism animates and energizes their ministry of reconciliation and, not unexpectedly, their encounter with the cross of separation. Thanks are due to so many for the possibility of the present publication but a special tribute of gratitude is surely in order to Mrs Pamela Gaughan for her outstanding translation of the Dombes Agreement.

Norwich 1973

ALAN C. CLARK
Bishop of Elmham

INTRODUCTION

Documents on Modern Eucharistic Agreement

Based on a lecture given on 27 May, 1972
at the Trinity Institute, New York

by H. R. McAdoo

*Bishop of Ossory, Ferns
and Leighlin*

INTRODUCTION

1

THE STATUS OF
THE ANGLICAN–ROMAN CATHOLIC
INTERNATIONAL COMMISSION'S
'AGREED STATEMENT ON CHRISTIAN DOCTRINE'

It may seem unnecessary, and even perverse, to begin an examination of this document by stating first what it is not, but the point of departure as well as the direction of the *Agreed Statement* is not unconnected with its status. The *Agreed Statement* is *not* an agreement which has been formally ratified by both Churches and handed down from on high as a directive, but its standing is more than that of a private essay by several hands. Its status is that of a consensus, a 'substantial agreement', arrived at by an international group of eighteen theologians, members of a Commission officially appointed by both Communions to inaugurate and continue that 'serious dialogue' between the two Churches which Pope Paul VI and the Archbishop of Canterbury announced their intention of bringing about in their *Common Declaration* of March 1966.

It will be recalled that the Joint Anglican–Roman Catholic Preparatory Commission was born of that *Declaration* and it made its report, now known as the *Malta Report*, early in 1968. Among the recommendations contained in it was one suggesting the setting up of a Joint Permanent Commission. This was done in 1969, the word 'permanent' being quietly replaced by the word 'international', since the implication of talking until the Parousia was not liked. The International Commission met at Venice in 1970 and shared its working papers with the general public, publishing these in 1971, so that the Church at large might know something of how the members saw their task. The *Agreed Statement* is the first-fruits of the Commission's labours; the

3

status of the document is therefore not unconnected with its aim and method.

While the document is not ecclesiastically binding, it has this much authority, that it is the considered consensus of a Commission officially appointed to do the work. Its findings, as Bishop B. C. Butler, one of its distinguished members has put it, 'are capable of being, and in the instance of the *Agreed Statement* on the eucharist, are likely to be historic steps on the road of mutual understanding between the two Churches, those "sisters" to whose eventual embrace within a single communion the Pope, in his sermon at the canonization of the Forty Martyrs, looked forward with hope'.[1] The Commission is not only international in its membership, but in its attitudes, and is representative of the "variety of theological approaches" which we acknowledge as existing 'within both our Communions'.[2]

The document should be read as a whole and in the light of the Commission's expressed intention. Much of the criticism which it has encountered seems to arise from readers taking sections or even sentences in isolation and from their approaching the document from the standpoint of medieval and sixteenth-century definitions and formularies, or even caricatures of these, rather than from the point at which the Commission began its journey. The criticism of the document has not all been adverse; much favourable and welcoming comment has also been made, not infrequently by members of Christian Churches who are not direct participants in this particular dialogue.

2
THE PURPOSE AND AIM OF THE 'AGREED STATEMENT'

'Our intention was to reach a consensus at the level of faith, so that all of us might be able to say, within the limits of the Statement: this is the Christian faith of the eucharist'.[3]

The Commission's aim was to produce a statement in which all could recognize not necessarily the confessional terminology with which they had been familiar, but the Christian faith of the eucharist as that has been given to the people of God: 'We have seen it as our task to find a way of advancing together beyond the doctrinal disagreements of the past'.[4]

Put in the simplest terms, the *Agreed Statement* strives to concentrate on the reality of the eucharist, on its purpose and meaning, on what it is for, and what it does within the common life of the body of Christ. It does not seek, after a later fashion, to make definitions or formulations of how the eucharist effects its purpose. It attempts to go back to an earlier Christian approach, believing that this is the only and providential way forward. It seeks to go back behind the divisive definitions of later times to Scripture, to the biblical realism, and to an earlier approach which it believes to be more consonant with Scripture as reflected, for example, in the words of John of Damascus: 'If you inquire as to the method, how this comes to be, it is enough for you to hear that it is by means of the Holy Ghost'.

The Commission therefore makes the following statement of its aim: 'Our intention has been to seek a deeper understanding of the reality of the eucharist which is consonant with biblical teaching and with the tradition of our common inheritance, and to express in this document the consensus we have reached' (para. 1).

It is hoped that what has been said in this section explains the purpose and the methodology of the *Agreed Statement* and justifies the assertion that possibly the most important aspect of it is the manner of its approach to the subject.[5]

3

COMMENTARY ON THE
'AGREED STATEMENT'

The commentary and analysis of the *Agreed Statement* which occupy most of the remainder of this introduction are those of an individual. We will now take a look at three other recent eucharistic documents for two reasons: first, their style of handling the question is broadly similar to that of the *Agreed Statement*; secondly, only two of these four are linked in any way. This in itself may well be a significant pointer and an encouragement to all Christians who desire to see the *sacrament* of unity once more as the sacrament of *unity*.

A. THE EUCHARIST: A LUTHERAN–ROMAN CATHOLIC STATEMENT

The text of this is available on pp. 33-49 of this book. It hails from the U.S.A. and is a fuller and more explanatory document, designed for a slightly different purpose, one would imagine, than that of the *Agreed Statement*. All we need to do is to note certain important resemblances of form and content. This statement falls into two parts, dealing with 'The Eucharist as Sacrifice' and 'The Presence of Christ in the Lord's Supper' respectively. This corresponds closely in form to the *Agreed Statement*, but possibly the greatest difference between the two documents lies in the style of the Lutheran–Roman Catholic essay which tends in part to proceed by way of a comparative evaluation of both traditions in respect of specific subjects. The Anglican–Roman Catholic document sets out to be what its title indicates, an *agreed* statement. But the similarity both in treatment and general conclusions is deserving of note. For example, the once-for-all character and completeness of the sacrifice of the cross is unequivocally and fully stated by both sets of conversationalists. In the same way, both statements relate the eucharist to the one sacrifice in terms not of a human recalling of past events, but of a divine making present, through the Holy Spirit, of these events in which the worshipper participates in Christ.

In the section on the presence, the Lutheran–Roman Catholic statement lists the affirmations which both sides can make concerning the presence which they affirm to be a real presence:

> Our traditions have spoken of this presence as 'sacramental', 'supernatural', and 'spiritual'. These terms have different connotations in the two traditions, but they have in common a rejection of a spatial or natural manner of presence, and a rejection of an understanding of the sacrament as only commemorative or figurative.

This is parallel to the *Agreed Statement*, as are most of the other affirmatives. Points of Lutheran–Roman Catholic divergence such as reservation for extra-liturgical purposes and the content of the word 'transubstantiation' are analysed from the Lutheran angle.

A short paragraph towards the end of the document (see p. 43 of this book) is very significant in that it implies the same kind of thinking as that which informs the *Agreed Statement* of the Anglican–Roman Catholic Commission:

> It can thus be seen that there is agreement on the 'that', the full reality of Christ's presence. What has been disputed is a particular way of stating the 'how', the manner in which he becomes present.

The document notes, as does the *Agreed Statement,* than when Lutherans read *contemporary* Roman Catholic expositions, 'it becomes clear to them that the dogma of transubstantiation intends to affirm the fact of Christ's presence and of the change which takes place, and is not an attempt to explain how Christ becomes present'. Lutheran rejection of transubstantiation as 'the one and only conceptual framework' and as 'a rationalistic attempt to explain the mystery' has already been noted. A chemical or physical change is rejected while a sacramental change is posited.

Having listed certain differences, the statement ends on a note of conviction that there is a growing convergence in the two traditions.

B. THE DOMBES AGREEMENT

Equally interesting is the work of the semi-official Groupe des Dombes, founded as far back as 1937 by the Abbé Paul Couturier, with a French Reformed and Roman Catholic membership. Their publication, *Towards a Common Eucharistic Faith?: Agreement between Catholics and Protestants,* a translation of which is to be found on pp. 51-78 of this book, is an agreed statement, or rather two agreed statements, a *Doctrinal Agreement* and a *Pastoral Agreement,* within a report and commentary. Once again, one is struck by the similarity of approach in this document.

The *Doctrinal Agreement* (para. 2) insists, like the *Agreed Statement* (para. 1), on substantial agreement concerning the reality of the eucharist 'despite theological divergences', as a preliminary to sharing at the Lord's Table.[6]

It is in the commentary at the end of the document that its rationale is set out.[7] Here one notes parallels and similarities with the *Agreed Statement*: it is a doctrinal agreement as to what is essential and a fresh approach is adopted which bears a resemblance to the International Commission's emphasis on the 'the reality of the eucharist' (*Agreed Statement,* para. 1). The French document notes:

> This we have endeavoured to do, seeking less to say what we regard as essential than to confess together with gratitude, the essential thing that he, Christ, gives us by making us share in his being and his life in the sacramental mystery of the Church.[8]

It is in relation to this concept of what is essential that the members of the Group in their dialogue have examined their respective standpoints,

> not in order to abandon them, but in order better to discern their real substance and hence their necessary reconciliation.[9]

The Dombes Agreement is 'a doctrinal agreement as to what is essential, with regard to the meaning of the eucharist and its significance for the Church'.[10] It is addressed in the first place to the authorities of both Churches in France and then to all Christians, as a contribution to the ongoing dialogue at all levels.

C. THE WCC STATEMENT: THE EUCHARIST IN ECUMENICAL THOUGHT

It will be convenient to combine here my comments on the *Doctrinal Agreement on the Eucharist* of the Dombes Group with those which I wish to make on the WCC Statement.

At the conference of the Faith and Order Commission of the World Council of Churches held at Louvain in August 1971, a consensus on the eucharist entitled *The Eucharist in Ecumenical Thought* was drawn up. Its text is to be found on pp. 79-89 of this book. If one compares this document with the Dombes Agreement, one sees an extensive identity of material in that

8

much of the contents of the seven paragraphs of the WCC consensus, as well as the title-headings, have their parallels in the statement of the Dombes Group. A two-way traffic here should, however, be noted, in that the Group's work

> was already known to the World Council of Churches at Geneva (Faith and Order Commission) as well as to the Roman Secretariat for Unity, by the intermediary of those of us who belonged to one or other of those bodies.[11]

The Faith and Order Commission's consensus was itself drawn up to implement a resolution passed at the Commission's meeting at Bristol in 1967:

> That there be drawn up a résumé of the emerging ecumenical consensus on the eucharist, drawing on the work of Lund, Montreal, Aarhus, and Bristol, and on the work of regional groups and of individual scholars related to the ecumenical discussion of the eucharist.[12]

The résumé was therefore based on paragraphs produced by the Third and Fourth World Conferences on Faith and Order at Lund in 1952 and Montreal in 1963 and by the Faith and Order Commission itself at Bristol in 1967 and which were contained in the official records.

> The substance of the paragraphs was produced by sections of these conferences, or of the Commission, which were broadly representative of the major confessional families. In every case, the section in turn had drawn upon the work of a theological or study commission that had laboured over several years, and upon the work of specialists in the field.[13]

The Dombes Agreement and the WCC Statement contain similar material and it is interesting to compare the title-headings:

THE DOMBES AGREEMENT
1. The eucharist: the Lord's supper
2. The eucharist: act of thanksgiving to the Father
3. The eucharist: memorial (*anamnesis*) of Christ
4. The eucharist: a gift of the Spirit
5. The sacramental presence of Christ

6. The eucharist: communion in the Body of Christ
7. The eucharist: a mission in the world
8. The eucharist: banquet of the Kingdom
9. The Presidency of the eucharist[14]

THE WCC STATEMENT
1. The eucharist: the Lord's supper
2. The eucharist: thanksgiving to the Father
3. The eucharist: memorial (*anamnesis*) of Christ
4. The eucharist: gift of the Spirit
5. The eucharist: communion of the Body of Christ
6. The eucharist: mission to the world
7. The eucharist: end of divisions[15]

Thus it will be seen that the WCC Statement lacks nos. 5, 8, and 9 of the Dombes Agreement. However, the central sentence of 5 is paralleled in paragraph 1 of the WCC Statement: 'The eucharistic meal is the sacrament of the body and blood of Christ, the sacrament of his real presence', and although the *Doctrinal Agreement* of the Dombes Group has no parallel to paragraph 7 of the WCC Statement, its equivalent may be seen in paragraph 7 of the *Pastoral Agreement*, 'The eucharist: source of unity'.

This inter-relation between the Dombes Agreement and the consensus of the Faith and Order Commission obviously widens the range and implications of the Dombes Agreement, and is referred to in the latter document, which is briefer and more condensed than the Faith and Order Commission's résumé. Like the International Commission, the Dombes Group wished to devote more space to the sacramental presence and the role of faith; there is indeed a noteworthy general closeness of major content as between the *Agreed Statement* and *Towards a Common Eucharistic Faith?*. For example, there is the treatment of the eucharist as memorial (*anamnesis*) of the totality of Christ's life and in particular, of his cross and resurrection, by which the Church proclaims the mighty acts of God, and re-presents to the Father the one perfect sacrifice of his Son, in union with whom we offer ourselves as a holy and living sacrifice expressed in our daily lives.[16] We may compare this with the *Agreed Statement*, paras. 3-5.

10

Again, there is the emphasis on the role of the Holy Spirit and on the eschatological banquet (see paras. 14, 15, 29-31, of the Dombes Agreement), which is paralleled in paragraphs 10, 11, and also 3 and 4 of the *Agreed Statement*.

The section on 'the sacramental presence of Christ' in paragraphs17-20 of the Dombes Agreement should be compared with paragraphs 6-10 of the *Agreed Statement*. There is unanimous agreement on the real presence—'the real living and effective presence of Christ in this sacrament' (para. 17 of the Dombes Agreement). The adjectives 'living' and 'active' are echoed in the *Agreed Statement,* which makes the same dynamic emphasis.

Both statements underline the vital role of faith and at the same time assert that:

> The presence of Christ revealed to his Church in the eucharist does not depend on the faith of the individual, for it is Christ who binds himself in his words and in the Spirit to the sacramental act, the sign of his giving of his presence.[17]

Like paragraph 10 of the *Agreed Statement,* the Dombes Agreement asserts the biblical realism:

> Christ's act being the gift of his body and blood, that is to say, of himself, the reality given in the signs of the bread and the wine is his body and his blood. It is by virtue of Christ's creative word and by the power of the Holy Spirit that the bread and wine are made a sacrament and hence a 'sharing of the body and blood of Christ' (1 Cor. 10.16). They are henceforth, in their ultimate truth, beneath the outward sign, the given reality and so they remain, that they may be consumed.[18]

Similarly, in the *Pastoral Agreement* on the meaning of the eucharist, the French colloquy asserts, 'this bread and this wine are thus the body and blood of Christ, given by him to his Church' (para. 3).

Like those who produced the Lutheran–Roman Catholic document, the Dombes Group insist in a footnote that the biblical realism, as I call it, implies neither a localized presence nor a physico-chemical change; they quote both Calvin and St

11

Thomas Aquinas to ensure fair play.[19] While the *Agreed Statement* does not spell this out, it is abundantly clear from the language of the Statement throughout that this point of view is accepted.

Again, the *Agreed Statement* and the *Doctrinal Agreement* of the Dombes Group lay stress on the relation of the eucharist to the Church's mission in the world and on the eschatological context of the eucharist.

Significantly, both publications affirm the belief of the participants that substantial agreement has been reached and the main difficulties removed.[20] The Dombes Group comment that reservation and the question of apostolic succession now need to be examined.[21] The International Commission has already embarked upon an examination of the subject of the ministry and the Dombes Group have now produced a little book entitled *Pour une réconciliation des ministères* (1973).

Both the statements are explicitly aware of the implications of the inexhaustible mystery of the eucharist.

A last comment on the Dombes Agreement might be—not inappropriately—*toujours de l'audace*! It contains the honest demand that the authorities of both Churches should now give attention to the new situation created by this agreement on the eucharist.[22] Clearly the Group does not suffer from that failure of nerve which seems to afflict many ecumenical theologians who come forward with a proposal but rapidly retreat if the Church at large shows any signs of taking it and them seriously!

I have dwelt on these three documents, the WCC Statement and the Dombes Agreement, because I believe that, taken in conjunction with the *Agreed Statement*, they constitute a movement of shared thought and prayer producing a type of approach which has clearly cut across confessional boundaries as well as the line of past disagreements, and which opens the way for a real ecumenical advance. One trusts that they will not disappear into the archives, but will become a spring-board for action. One wonders whether we have as yet grasped the potential in the fact that groups of Roman Catholics, Anglicans, Lutherans, and

12

members of the French Reformed Church have found themselves moving with honesty and conviction in the same general direction.

The International Commission did not attempt any explanation of the *Agreed Statement*, but when one looks at the Dombes Agreement with its commentary, one wonders whether they took the right decision. At any rate I shall now attempt a selective commentary on a few aspects of the *Agreed Statement*, which must be taken as an expression of my own personal views.

The documents which we have been discussing and which are published in this book all illustrate an older approach to the eucharist which has always been the view of a majority of classical Anglican theologians. Hooker's words might well serve as an introduction to the thinking which informs them:

> Shall I wish that men would give themselves more to meditate with silence what we have by the sacrament, and less to dispute of the manner How?[23]

This is in fact the line taken by Lancelot Andrewes in his *Responsio*:

> Christ said, 'This is my Body'. He did not say, 'This is my Body in this way.' We are in agreement with you as to the end; the whole controversy is as to the method . . . and because there is no word, we rightly make it not of faith; we place it perhaps among the theories of the Schools, but not among the articles of the faith . . . we believe no less than you that the presence is real. Concerning the method of the presence, we define nothing rashly. . . .[24]

The same approach is found in John Bramhall,[25] and it is thoroughly representative of a great deal of Anglican thinking on the subject. Neither does the *Agreed Statement* define it, but it describes the eucharistic presence as a mystery (para. 8; cf. paras. 3, 6). It is a striking indication of direction that these twentieth-century eucharistic statements evidently regard this question from a similar standpoint.

In the same way, by its terminology as much as by its whole

13

form and content, the *Agreed Statement* makes it clear (to any who may still have their lingering suspicions) that there is no question here of a localized material presence, e.g., 'his sacramental presence given through bread and wine', 'gives himself sacramentally in the body and blood of his paschal sacrifice', 'the sacramental body and blood of the Saviour are present as an offering to the believer awaiting his welcome'. Note also paragraph 11:

> The Lord who thus comes to his people in the power of the Holy Spirit is the Lord of glory. In the eucharistic celebration we anticipate the joys of the age to come. By the transforming action of the Spirit of God, earthly bread and wine become the heavenly manna and the new wine, the eschatological banquet for the new man: elements of the first creation become pledges and first fruits of the new heaven and the new earth.

'What we have by the Sacrament', to use Hooker's phrase, is the controlling element in the *Agreed Statement*. You meet it, under its various aspects, in paragraphs 1 to 4, and it recurs in one shape or another elsewhere. In paragraph 6 it is put succintly:

> Its purpose is to transmit the life of the crucified and risen Christ to his body, the Church, so that its members may be more fully united with Christ and with one another.

As I have written elsewhere:

> It is therefore the reality of the eucharist, its purpose, and what it does within the *koinonia* which constitutes the primary matter for agreement. It is Christ, living and giving himself to his people, building them up and transforming them: 'As the living Father sent me, and I live because of the Father, so he who eats me shall live because of me' (Jn 6.57).[26]

Indeed it is no accident that St Thomas Aquinas, describing the meaning of the eucharist, quotes this same verse and says:

> The effect of this sacrament ought to be considered, first of all and principally, from what is contained in this sacrament,

which is Christ; who . . . also, by coming sacramentally into man, causes the life of grace, according to John 6.58: 'He that eateth me, the same also shall live by me.'[27]

The *Agreed Statement* uses the phrase, previously quoted, 'its purpose is to transmit the life' of Christ to the members of his body. So Hooker also:

Life being therefore proposed unto all men as their end, they which by baptism have laid the foundation and attained the first beginning of a new life have here their nourishment and food prescribed for continuance of life in them. Such as will live the life of God must eat the flesh and drink the blood of the Son of man, because this is a part of that diet which if we want we cannot live.[28]

Precisely the same theme occurs in Jeremy Taylor's *Worthy Communicant*:

The sum is this: Christ's body, his flesh and blood, are therefore called our meat and drink, because by his incarnation and manifestation in the flesh he became life to us; so that it is mysterious indeed in the expression, but very proper and intelligible in the event, to say that we eat his flesh and drink his blood, *since by these it is that we have* and preserve life.[29]

Is there not something prophetic in the irenic and discerning words of Hooker, referring to the fear that

men should account of this sacrament but only as of a shadow, destitute, empty, and void of Christ. But seeing that by opening the several opinions which have been held, they are grown for aught I can see on all sides at length to a general agreement. . . .

And what, in Hooker's view, is that agreement? Let him answer for himself:

. . . a general agreement concerning that which alone is material, namely the *real participation* of Christ and of life in his body and blood by means of this sacrament.[30]

Set over against the form and content of the four modern eucharistic agreements, we must surely grant that this is a proleptic phrase.

This presence of Christ, this coming to his people, and what the *Agreed Statement* (para. 8) calls 'a lifegiving encounter' which results when met by faith, is at the heart of that document. In this connection we should note that there is a dynamic approach in the *Agreed Statement* to the presence, which is very relevant to the movement of Christians towards a common understanding of the eucharist. 'Christ is present and active', says the *Agreed Statement* (para. 7), and it is apposite to recall a sentence from one of the published Venice working-papers out of which, among other background material, the *Agreed Statement* evolved:

> The real presence of the risen Christ in the elements, as understood in the Western Catholic tradition, should be seen as a dynamic presence, finding its fulfilment in the unity of the body of Christ and in the sanctification of the believer.[31]

Catholic and Evangelical come closest together at this point, I believe, in recognizing that *Christ present means Christ active*. That standard Anglican of the early decades of this century, E. J. Bicknell, was well ahead of his time—as theologians sometimes tend to be if they get at the heart of things—when he wrote:

> Let us admit that the primary idea of the eucharist is that of Christ active rather than of Christ present, of Christ as bestowing a gift rather than of the gift bestowed. But it still remains true that our imaginations are unable to conceive of Christ as active unless he is in some sense present and of the gift as bestowed unless it is there to be bestowed.[32]

Within this context of a dynamic presence, of a lifegiving encounter, and of faith, it seems to me that there are two, and only two, radical questions to be asked and answered:

1. What is the purpose of receiving the body and blood of Christ? (Or, what do people expect to happen when they come to Holy Communion?)

2. What meaning, what reality, is intended to be conveyed by

the words 'body' and 'blood', both at the institution of the eucharist and at every subsequent celebration of it?

If we pose and answer these questions along the lines of these three documents of our times—and in the spirit of Aquinas, Hooker, and Taylor—we must see, I believe, that it is not a *thing* about which we are talking, but a *Life,* the Life of Christ. In the words of paragraph 3 of the *Agreed Statement*:

> Christ . . . in the eucharist builds up the life of the Church, strengthens its fellowship, and furthers its mission. . . . In the whole action of the eucharist, and in and by his sacramental presence given through bread and wine, the crucified and risen Lord, according to his promise, offers himself to his people.

This thought is amplified in paragraph 7, which sees the whole eucharistic action as uniquely expressing Christ's living activity, as consecrator as well as in the sacramental gift, as proclaimed and as proclaiming, as immanent 'in the entire eucharistic celebration' and as 'transcending the sacramental order':

> Christ is present and active in various ways, in the entire eucharistic celebration. It is the same Lord who through the proclaimed word invites his people to his table, who through his minister presides at that table, and who gives himself sacramentally in the body and blood of his paschal sacrifice. It is the Lord present at the right hand of the Father, and therefore transcending the sacramental order, who thus offers to his Church, in the eucharistic signs, the special gift of himself.

Such a profession of belief seems to me to combine in its wholeness of truth all that Catholics and Evangelicals have striven to express. Particularly must this be felt to be so when they read what paragraph 8 has to say about the role of faith and about 'the personal relationship between Christ and the faithful', and what paragraph 9 notes concerning the unity of the one liturgical action:

> The Lord's words at the last supper, 'Take and eat; this is

17

my body', do not allow us to dissociate the gift of the presence and the act of sacramental eating.

I conclude with a short comment on Section II of the *Agreed Statement*, The Eucharist and the Sacrifice of Christ. It is a moving out past ideas such as 'resacrificing Christ', past ideas such as that there can be no legitimate place in eucharistic theology for sacrificial language, past subtler refinements of both, into a different, clearer atmosphere. There are signs that thinking on the subject in both Communions is now recasting itself in another form, that of a sacred meal within which a memorial is made of the unique and unrepeatable self-offering of Christ, and that which happened once for all is made 'effective in the present' and 'made effective in the life of the Church' (para. 5). As 'the atoning work of Christ on the cross' is made effective, so first, is it 'proclaimed' in the eucharist, and 'his members . . . participate in these benefits and enter into the movement of his self-offering' (para. 5).

All words and formulations fail utterly to capture and crystallize the range of Christian thought and experience here. This is impossible, but there is in this section an attempt to be true to those words of Scripture which we know so well that sometimes we do not hear their undertones until something like the *Agreed Statement*, inadequate as it is, brings into their true juxtaposition thoughts such as 'memorial', 'sacrifice', and 'proclamation':

> For the tradition which I handed on to you came to me from the Lord himself: that the Lord Jesus, on the night of his arrest, took bread, and, after giving thanks to God, broke it and said: 'This is my body which is for you; do this as a memorial of me.' In the same way, he took the cup after supper, and said: 'This cup is the new covenant sealed by my blood. Whenever you drink it, do this as a memorial of me.' For every time you eat this bread and drink the cup, you proclaim the death of the Lord, until he comes (1 Cor. 11. 23–36 NEB).

We may compare with this the Dutch Catechism:

We join in with the one sacrifice—especially by eating.
The repast and the sacrifice are not to be separated.
The sacrifice is a repast. . . .[33]

Thus the *Agreed Statement* sums it up:

Christ instituted the eucharist as a memorial (*anamnesis*) of
the totality of God's reconciling action in him (para. 5).

The position is well summed up by two famous hymns:

With solemn faith we offer up
And spread before thy glorious eyes
That only ground of all our hope,
That one eternal sacrifice,
Which brings thy grace on sinners down,
And perfects all our souls in one.[34]

This is answered by Bright's great Anglican eucharistic hymn:

And now, O Father, mindful of the love
That bought us, once for all, on Calvary's Tree
And having with us him that pleads above,
We here present, we here spread forth to thee,
That only Offering perfect in thine eyes,
The one true, pure, immortal Sacrifice.

Thinking on this subject is now tending to recast itself in another
form, but this does not imply that this is a new form, for it is
there in outline in hymnody. It is spelled out for his own times
by Jeremy Taylor:

And this also his ministers do on earth. They offer up the
same Sacrifice to God, the Sacrifice of the cross by prayers,
and a commemorating rite and representment, according to
his holy institution. . . . As Christ is a priest in heaven for
ever and yet does not sacrifice himself afresh nor yet without
a Sacrifice could he be a priest, but by a daily ministration
and intercession represents his sacrifice to God and offers himself as sacrificed, so he does upon earth by the ministry of his
servants. He is offered to God; that is, he is by prayers and

the sacrament represented or offered up to God as sacrificed, which in effect is a celebration of his death, and the applying of it to the present and future necessities of the Church as we are capable by a ministry like his in heaven. It follows, then, that the celebration of this Sacrifice be in its proportion an instrument of applying the proper Sacrifice to all the purposes which it first designed.[35]

In conclusion, it is my belief that the *Agreed Statement* represents a lead forward, and one which we trust will be followed by the Church at large, going into committee at every level so that we may learn whether the people of God endorse this agreement and desire that action should follow. In itself, and in the expressed view of its compilers, it is a modest document, and not 'a comprehensive treatment of the subject' (Introduction). But we stand by the assertions that 'nothing essential has been omitted', that it is 'a substantial agreement' (para. 12), and that 'if there are any remaining points of disagreement they can be resolved on the principles here established'.[36]

HENRY OSSORY

NOTES

References to pages in this book are in brackets, thus [   ].

1. B. C. Butler in *The Tablet*, 8 January 1972
2. *Agreed Statement*, para. 12
3. Ibid., Introduction
4. Ibid., para. 12
5. See H. R. McAdoo, 'The Significance of the Windsor Agreement', in *Church Times*, 31 December 1971.
6. Cf. *The Lambeth Conference* (1968): *Resolutions and Reports*, p. 128: 'Whenever intercommunion is proposed between Churches, we believe that there should first be found a basic agreement on the meaning of the eucharist'.
7. See [p. 67-77]
8. Dombes Agreement, *Commentary*, para. 3 [p. 69-70]
9. Ibid. [p. 70]
10. Ibid., para. 1, cf. *Agreed Statement*, Introduction
11. Dombes Agreement, Introduction [p. 55]; cf. *Commentary*, para. 2 [pp. 68-9]

12. [p. 81]. For further documentation see *Istina,* 16(1971), no.3, pp. 369-73.
13. [p. 81-2]
14. Title-headings on [pp. 57-62]
15. Title-headings on [pp. 83-7]
16. *Doctrinal Agreement,* Section III [pp. 58-9]
17. Ibid., Section ff, para. 18 [pp. 59-60]; cf. *Agreed Statement,* para. 8
18. Ibid., para. 19 [p. 60]
19. [p. 77 n 2]
20. *Doctrinal Agreement,* paras. 36-7 [p. 63]; *Agreed Statement,* para. 12 [p. 29]
21. *Doctrinal Agreement,* para. 37 [p. 63]; cf. *Lutheran–Roman Catholic Statement,* Conclusion [p. 43]
22. Para. 40 [p. 64]
23. *Ecclesiastical Polity,* V, lxvii, 3
24. *Responsio ad apologiam Cardinalis Bellarmine* [C. I. 1] (1610)
25. *An Answer to M. de la Milletière,* in *Works,* L.A.C.T. edn, Vol. 1, pp. 7-8
26. *Church Times,* 31 December 1971
27. *S.T.,* III, Q79, A1
28. *E.P.,* V, lxvii, 1
29. Section III
30. *E.P.,* V, lxvii, 2
31. The Venice working documents were published in *Theology* and *The Clergy Review,* February 1971.
32. *A Theological Introduction to the Thirty-nine Articles* (1919), repr. 1936, p. 495
33. *A New Catechism* (E.T., 1967), p. 340
34. Quoted in A. M. Allchin, *Eucharist and Unity* (1972), p. 7
35. *The Great Exemplar* (1649), Pt III xv, discourse XIV
36. On the implications of the term 'substantial agreement', see J. M. R. Tillard, OP [a member of the International Commision], 'Anglican–Roman Catholic Dialogue', in *One in Christ,* VIII (1972), no. 3.

AN
AGREED STATEMENT
ON EUCHARISTIC
DOCTRINE

Anglican–Roman Catholic
International Commission

WINDSOR 1971

First published in 1972 by S.P.C.K.

INTRODUCTION

The following Agreed Statement evolved from the thinking and the discussion of the Anglican–Roman Catholic International Commission over the past two years. The result has been a conviction among members of the Commission that we have reached agreement on essential points of eucharistic doctrine. We are equally convinced ourselves that, though no attempt was made to present a fully comprehensive treatment of the subject, nothing essential has been omitted. The document agreed upon at our third meeting, at Windsor, on 7 September 1971, has been presented to our official authorities, but obviously it cannot be ratified by them until such time as our respective Churches can evaluate its conclusions.

We would want to point out that the members of the Commission who subscribed to this Statement have been officially appointed and come from many countries, representing a wide variety of theological background. Our intention was to reach a consensus at the level of faith, so that all of us might be able to say, within the limits of the Statement: this is the Christian faith of the eucharist.

HENRY OSSORY
ALAN ELMHAM
Co-Chairmen

THE STATEMENT

1. In the course of the Church's history several traditions have developed in expressing Christian understanding of the eucharist. (For example, various names have become customary as descriptions of the eucharist: Lord's supper, liturgy, holy mysteries, synaxis, mass, holy communion. The eucharist has become the most universally accepted term.) An important stage in progress towards organic unity is a substantial consensus on the purpose and meaning of the eucharist. Our intention has been to seek a deeper understanding of the reality of the eucharist which is consonant with biblical teaching and with the tradition of our common inheritance, and to express in this document the consensus we have reached.

2. Through the life, death and resurrection of Jesus Christ God has reconciled men to himself, and in Christ he offers unity to all mankind. By his word God calls us into a new relationship with himself as our Father and with one another as his children —a relationship inaugurated by baptism into Christ through the Holy Spirit, nurtured and deepened through the eucharist, and expressed in a confession of one faith and a common life of loving service.

I THE MYSTERY OF THE EUCHARIST

3. When his people are gathered at the eucharist to commemorate his saving acts for our redemption, Christ makes effective among us the eternal benefits of his victory and elicits and renews our response of faith, thanksgiving and self-surrender. Christ through the Holy Spirit in the eucharist builds up the life of the Church, strengthens its fellowship and furthers its mission. The identity of the Church as the body of Christ is both expressed and effectively proclaimed by its being centred in, and partaking of, his body and blood. In the whole action of the eucharist, and in and by his sacramental presence given through

bread and wine, the crucified and risen Lord, according to his promise, offers himself to his people.

4. In the eucharist we proclaim the Lord's death until he comes. Receiving a foretaste of the kingdom to come, we look back with thanksgiving to what Christ has done for us, we greet him present among us, we look forward to his final appearing in the fulness of his kingdom when 'The Son also himself (shall) be subject unto him that put all things under him, that God may be all in all' (1 Cor. 15.28). When we gather around the same table in this communal meal at the invitation of the same Lord and when we 'partake of the one loaf', we are one in commitment not only to Christ and to one another, but also to the mission of the Church in the world.

II The Eucharist and the Sacrifice of Christ

5. Christ's redeeming death and resurrection took place once and for all in history. Christ's death on the cross, the culmination of his whole life of obedience, was the one, perfect and sufficient sacrifice for the sins of the world. There can be no repetition of or addition to what was then accomplished once for all by Christ. Any attempt to express a nexus between the sacrifice of Christ and the eucharist must not obscure this fundamental fact of the Christian faith.[1] Yet God has given the eucharist to his Church as a means through which the atoning work of Christ on the cross is proclaimed and made effective in the life of the Church. The notion of *memorial* as understood in the passover celebration at the time of Christ—i.e., the making effective in the present of an event in the past—has opened the way to a clearer understanding of the relationship between Christ's sacrifice and the eucharist. The eucharistic memorial is no mere calling to mind of a past event or of its significance, but the Church's effectual proclamation of God's mighty acts. Christ instituted the eucharist as a memorial (*anamnesis*) of the totality of God's reconciling action in him. In the eucharistic prayer the Church continues to make a perpetual memorial of Christ's death, and his members, united with God and one another, give thanks for all his mercies, entreat the benefits of

27

his passion on behalf of the whole Church, participate in these benefits and enter into the movement of his self-offering.

III The Presence of Christ

6. Communion with Christ in the eucharist presupposes his true presence, effectually signified by the bread and wine which, in this mystery, become his body and blood.[2] The real presence of his body and blood can, however, only be understood within the context of the redemptive activity whereby he gives himself, and in himself reconciliation, peace and life, to his own. On the one hand, the eucharistic gift springs out of the paschal mystery of Christ's death and resurrection, in which God's saving purpose, has already been definitely realized. On the other hand, its purpose is to transmit the life of the crucified and risen Christ to his body, the Church, so that its members may be more fully united with Christ and with one another.

7. Christ is present and active, in various ways, in the entire eucharistic celebration. It is the same Lord who through the proclaimed word invites his people to his table, who through his minister presides at that table, and who gives himself sacramentally in the body and blood of his paschal sacrifice. It is the Lord present at the right hand of the Father, and therefore transcending the sacramental order, who thus offers to his Church, in the eucharistic signs, the special gift of himself.

8. The sacramental body and blood of the Saviour are present as an offering to the believer awaiting his welcome. When this offering is met by faith, a lifegiving encounter results. Through faith Christ's presence—which does not depend on the individual's faith in order to be the Lord's real gift of himself to his Church—becomes no longer just a presence *for* the believer, but also a presence *with* him. Thus, in considering the mystery of the eucharistic presence, we must recognize both the sacramental sign of Christ's presence and the personal relationship between Christ and the faithful which arises from that presence.

9. The Lord's words at the last supper, 'Take and eat; this is my body', do not allow us to dissociate the gift of the presence and the act of sacramental eating. The elements are not mere signs; Christ's body and blood become really present and are

28

really given. But they are really present and given in order that, receiving them, believers may be united in communion with Christ the Lord.

10. According to the traditional order of the liturgy the consecratory prayer (*anaphora*) leads to the communion of the faithful. Through this prayer of thanksgiving, a word of faith addressed to the Father, the bread and wine become the body and blood of Christ by the action of the Holy Spirit, so that in communion we eat the flesh of Christ and drink his blood.

11. The Lord who thus comes to his people in the power of the Holy Spirit is the Lord of glory. In the eucharistic celebration we anticipate the joys of the age to come. By the transforming action of the Spirit of God, earthly bread and wine become the heavenly manna and the new wine, the eschatological banquet for the new man: elements of the first creation become pledges and first fruits of the new heaven and the new earth.

---

12. We believe that we have reached substantial agreement on the doctrine of the eucharist. Although we are all conditioned by the traditional ways in which we have expressed and practised our eucharistic faith, we are convinced that if there are any remaining points of disagreement they can be resolved on the principles here established. We acknowledge a variety of theological approaches within both our communions. But we have seen it as our task to find a way of advancing together beyond the doctrinal disagreements of the past. It is our hope that, in view of the agreement which we have reached on eucharistic faith, this doctrine will no longer constitute an obstacle to the unity we seek.

MEMBERS OF THE COMMISSION

Those taking part in the Conversations were as follows:

ANGLICAN DELEGATES

The Rt Revd H. R. McAdoo, Bishop of Ossory, Ferns, and Leighlin (Co-Chairman)

The Most Revd F. A. Arnott, Archbishop of Brisbane

The Rt Revd J. R. H. Moorman, Bishop of Ripon

The Rt Revd E. G. Knapp-Fisher, Bishop of Pretoria

The Rt Revd A. A. Vogel, Bishop Co-adjutor of West Missouri

The Very Revd Henry Chadwick, Dean of Christ Church, Oxford

The Revd J. W. Charley, Vice-Principal, St John's College, Nottingham

The Revd Dr Eugene Fairweather, Keble Professor of Divinity, Trinity College, University of Toronto

The Revd Canon H. E. Root, Professor of Theology, University of Southampton

CONSULTANTS

The Revd Dr R. J. Halliburton, Vice-Principal of St Stephen's House, Oxford

The Revd Dr H. R. Smythe, Director, Anglican Centre, Rome

SECRETARY

The Revd Colin Davey, Assistant General Secretary, Church of England Council on Foreign Relations

ROMAN CATHOLIC DELEGATES

The Rt Revd Alan Clark, Auxiliary Bishop of Northampton (Co-Chairman)

The Rt Revd Christopher Butler, OSB, Auxiliary Bishop of Westminster

The Revd Fr Barnabas Ahern, CP, Professor of Sacred Scripture, Rome (Not at Windsor)

The Revd Fr P. Duprey, WF, Under Secretary, Vatican Secretariat for Promoting Christian Unity

The Revd Fr Herbert Ryan, SJ, Professor of Historical Theology, Pontifical Faculty of Theology, Woodstock College, New York

Professor J. J. Scarisbrick, Professor of History, University of Warwick

The Revd Fr Georges Tavard, AA, Professor of Theology, Methodist Theological School, Delaware, Ohio

The Revd Fr Jean M. Tillard, OP, Professor of Dogmatic Theology in the Dominican Faculty of Theology (Ottawa) and in Brussels

The Revd Fr E. J. Yarnold, SJ, Master, Campion Hall, Oxford

CONSULTANT

The Revd Fr Eugene Schallert, SJ, Director of the Institute for Socio-Religious Research, University of San Francisco

SECRETARY

The Very Revd Canon W. A. Purdy, Staff Member of the Vatican Secretariat for Promoting Christian Unity

WORLD COUNCIL OF CHURCHES OBSERVER

The Revd Dr Gunther Gassmann, Research Professor at the Centre d'Etudes Oecuméniques, Strasbourg

NOTES

1. The early Church in expressing the meaning of Christ's death and resurrection often used the language of sacrifice. For the Hebrew *sacrifice* was a traditional means of communication with God. The passover, for example, was a communal meal; the day of Atonement was essentially expiatory; and the covenant established communion between God and man.

2. The word *transubstantiation* is commonly used in the Roman Catholic Church to indicate that God acting in the eucharist effects a change in the inner reality of the elements. The term should be seen as affirming the *fact* of Christ's presence and of the mysterious and radical change which takes place. In contemporary Roman Catholic theology it is not understood as explaining *how* the change takes place.

31

THE
EUCHARIST AS
SACRIFICE

*A Lutheran—Roman Catholic
Statement*

ST LOUIS, MISSOURI, 1967

Extracted from *Lutherans and Catholics in Dialogue*

Published jointly by U.S.A. National Committee of the Lutheran World Federation and the Bishops' Committee for Ecumenical and Interreligious Affairs 1967.

INTRODUCTION

This statement is extracted from the third booklet in a series published in connection with theological dialogues held between representatives of the U.S. Catholic Bishops' Committee for Ecumenical and Interreligious Affairs and the U.S.A. National Committee of the Lutheran World Federation. It is entitled *III, The Eucharist as Sacrifice.* (The two earlier booklets were *I, The Status of the Nicene Creed as Dogma* and *II, One Baptism for the Remission of Sins.*)

Three meetings were devoted to the examination of this issue: 23-25 September 1966 at Washington D.C.; 7-9 April 1967 at New York; and 29 September-1 October 1967 at St Louis, Missouri. The third meeting was devoted almost entirely to the statement which follows.

The participants, a list of whom appears on pp. 44-5, wish it to be emphasized that although they were appointed by their sponsoring groups, they speak only on their own behalf and that their findings are in no way binding upon the groups which they represent.

THE EUCHARIST
A Lutheran–Roman Catholic
Statement

As a result of our conversations on the eucharist, we Roman Catholic and Lutheran theologians wish to record, chiefly and first of all, our profound gratitude to God for the growing unity on this subject which we see in our day.

Our responsibility is to try to articulate and explain this increasing agreement to the people and leadership of our Churches, so that they may test for themselves what we have discussed and draw whatever conclusions in thought and action they find appropriate.

What we have to report is not so much original with us as simply one manifestation of a growing consensus among many Christian traditions on the Lord's supper.[1]

Ours, however, is a specifically Roman Catholic–Lutheran contribution. It attempts to go beyond the more general ecumenical discussion of the eucharist to an examination of the particular agreements and disagreements of our two traditions. While we have considered the biblical and patristic sources of eucharistic doctrine and practice in our preparatory conversations, this statement deals with problems that have become particularly acute for Lutherans and Roman Catholics as a result of the sixteenth-century controversies. It does not try to treat the sacrament of the altar comprehensively.

Our attention has focused on two issues: the eucharist as sacrifice, and the presence of Christ in the sacrament. These issues have been especially divisive in the past and are involved in most of our historical disagreements on eucharistic doctrine and practice. For this reason it seems to us important to enunciate our growing agreement on these two points, even though there are other aspects of the sacrament of the altar we have not yet discussed.

I

THE EUCHARIST AS SACRIFICE[2]

With reference to the eucharist as sacrifice, two affirmations have not been denied by either confession; four aspects of the problem have been major points of divergence.

1. (a) Lutherans and Roman Catholics alike acknowledge that in the Lord's supper 'Christ is present as the Crucified who died for our sins and who rose again for our justification, as the once-for-all sacrifice for the sins of the world who gives himself to the faithful'.[3] On this Lutherans insist as much as Catholics, although, for various reasons, Lutherans have been reticent about speaking of the eucharist as a sacrifice.

   (b) The confessional documents of both traditions agree that the celebration of the eucharist is the Church's sacrifice of praise and self-offering or oblation. Each tradition can make the following statement its own: 'By him, with him and in him who is our great High Priest and Intercessor we offer to the Father, in the power of the Holy Spirit, our praise, thanksgiving and intercession. With contrite hearts we offer ourselves as a living and holy sacrifice, a sacrifice which must be expressed in the whole of our daily lives'.[4]

2. Historically, our controversies have revolved around the question whether the worshipping assembly 'offers Christ' in the sacrifice of the mass. In general, Lutherans have replied in the negative, because they believed that only thus could they preserve the once-for-all character and the full sufficiency of the sacrifice of the cross and keep the eucharist from becoming a human supplement to God's saving work, a matter of 'works-righteousness'.

   (a) First of all, we must be clear that Catholics as well as Lutherans affirm the unrepeatable character of the sacrifice of the cross. The Council of Trent, to be sure, affirmed this, but Lutheran doubts about the Catholic position were not resolved. Today, however, we find no

37

reason for such doubt, and we recognize our agreement in the assertion that 'What God did in the incarnation, life, death, resurrection, and ascension of Christ, he does not do again. The events are unique; they cannot be repeated, or extended or continued. Yet in this memorial we do not only recall past events: God makes them present through the Holy Spirit, thus making us participants in Christ' (1 Cor. 1.9).[5]

(b) Further, the Catholic affirmation that the Church 'offers Christ' in the mass has in the course of the last half century been increasingly explained in terms which answer Lutheran fears that this detracts from the full sufficiency of Christ's sacrifice. The members of the body of Christ are united through Christ with God and with one another in such a way that they become participants in his worship, his self-offering, his sacrifice to the Father. Through this union between Christ and Christians, the eucharistic assembly 'offers Christ' by consenting in the power of the Holy Spirit to be offered by him to the Father.[6] Apart from Christ we have no gifts, no worship, no sacrifice of our own to offer to God. All we can plead is Christ, the sacrificial lamb and victim whom the Father himself has given us.

(c) Another historically important point of controversy has been the Roman Catholic position that the eucharistic sacrifice is 'propitiatory'. Within the context of the emphases which we have outlined above, Catholics today interpret this position as emphatically affirming that the presence of the unique propitiatory sacrifice of the cross in the eucharistic celebration of the Church is efficacious for the forgiveness of sins and the life of the world. Lutherans can join them up to this point.[7] They reject, however, what they have understood Trent to say about the mass as a propitiatory sacrifice 'offered for the living and the dead',[8] even though the Apology of the Augsburg Confession concedes with respect to prayer for the dead that 'we do not forbid it'.[9] We have not discussed this

38

aspect of the problem; further exploration of it is required.

(d) In addition to the growing harmony in ways of thinking about the eucharistic sacrifice, there is a significant convergence in the actual practice of eucharistic worship. Doctrine is inevitably interpreted in the light of practice, as well as vice versa, and consequently oppositions on this level can negate apparent doctrinal agreement. For example, the Reformers and later Lutherans have believed that the multiplication of private masses and the associated systems of mass intentions and mass stipends are evidence that Roman Catholics do not take seriously the all-sufficiency of Christ's sacrifice, and this suspicion has been reinforced by such statements of Catholic theologians as 'the sacrificial worth of two Masses is just double the sacrificial worth of one Mass'.[10] Now, however, the Second Vatican Council in its Constitution on the Sacred Liturgy has declared that the nature of the mass is such that the communal way of celebrating is to be preferred to individual and quasi-private celebrations.[11] As the liturgical renewal progresses in this and other respects, each group in these discussions finds it increasingly easy to understand and approve what the other says about the eucharist in general and its sacrificial aspects in particular.

The question of eucharistic sacrifice is closely related to other issues. The problem of the 'real presence' has been the first to claim our attention. Do we, in the eucharist, genuinely encounter Christ in the full reality of his person and sacrificial action? It is therefore to this subject that we now turn.

II
THE PRESENCE OF CHRIST
IN THE LORD'S SUPPER

Here, too, there are areas in which this group believes that Roman Catholics and Lutherans can make the same affirmations, and others in which our agreement is not yet complete.

39

1. (a) We confess a manifold presence of Christ, the Word of God and Lord of the world. The crucified and risen Lord is present in his body, the people of God, for he is present where two or three are gathered in his name (Mt. 18.20). He is present in baptism, for it is Christ himself who baptizes.[12] He is present in the reading of the Scriptures and the proclamation of the gospel. He is present in the Lord's supper.[13]

   (b) We affirm that in the sacrament of the Lord's supper Jesus Christ, true God and true man, is present wholly and entirely in his body and blood, under the signs of bread and wine.[14]

   (c) Through the centuries Christians have attempted various formulations to describe this presence. Our confessional documents have in common affirmed that Jesus Christ is 'really', 'truly', and 'substantially' present in this sacrament.[15] This manner of presence ' we can scarcely express in words',[16] but we affirm his presence because we believe in the power of God and the promise of Jesus Christ, 'This is my body. . . . This is my blood. . . .'[17] Our traditions have spoken of this presence as 'sacramental',[18] 'supernatural', and 'spiritual'.[19] These terms have different connotations in the two traditions, but they have in common a rejection of a spatial or natural manner of presence, and a rejection of an understanding of the sacrament as only commemorative or figurative.[20] The term 'sign', once suspect, is again recognized as a positive term for speaking of Christ's presence in the sacrament.[21] For, though symbols and symbolic actions are used, the Lord's supper is an effective sign: it communicates what it promises; '. . . the action of the Church becomes the effective means whereby God in Christ acts and Christ is present with his people'.[22]

   (d) Although the sacrament is meant to be celebrated in the midst of the believing congregation, we are agreed that the presence of Christ does not come about through the faith of the believer, or through any human power, but by the power of the Holy Spirit through the word.[23]

(e) The true body and blood of Christ are present not only at the moment of reception but throughout the eucharistic action.[24]

2. In the following areas our historical divergences are being overcome, although we are unable at present to speak with one voice at every point.

(a) In reference to eucharistic worship:

a. We agreed that Christ gave us this sacrament in order that we might receive him and participate in his worship of the Father.[26]

b. We are also agreed that the Lord Jesus Christ is himself to be worshipped, praised, and adored; every knee is to bow before him.[26]

c. We are further agreed that as long as Christ remains sacramentally present, worship, reverence and adoration are appropriate.[27]

d. Both Lutherans and Catholics link Christ's eucharistic presence closely to the eucharistic liturgy itself. Lutherans, however, have not stressed the prolongation of this presence beyond the communion service as Catholics have done.

e. To be sure, the opposition on this point is not total. Following a practice attested in the early Church, Lutherans may distribute the elements from the congregational communion service to the sick in private communion, in some cases as an extension of this service, in some cases with the words of institution spoken either for their proclamatory value or as consecration.

f. Also in harmony with a eucharistic practice attested in the early Church, Roman Catholics have traditionally reserved the consecrated host for communicating the sick, which, according to the Instruction of 25 May 1967, is the 'primary and original purpose' of reservation.[28]. The adoration of Christ present in the reserved sacrament is of later origin and is a secondary end.[29] The same Instruction repeats the insistence of the Constitution on the Sacred Liturgy that any adoration of the reserved sacra-

41

ment be harmonized with and in some way derived from the liturgy, 'since the liturgy by its very nature surpasses' any nonliturgical eucharistic devotion.[30]

(b) In reference to the presence of Christ under both species, a divergence of practice concerning the cup for the laity has been one of the most obvious signs of disunity between Roman Catholics and other Christians. Catholics of the Eastern rites in union with the Roman See have always retained the practice of communion under both species. The Lutheran confessions emphasize the desirability of communion in both kinds in obedience to 'a clear command and order of Christ',[31] but do not deny the sacramental character of communion administered to a congregation in one kind only. At Vatican II the Roman Catholic Church reintroduced, to a modest but significant extent, communion under both kinds for the Western church.[32] The Council thereby recognized that this practice better expresses the sign of the mystery of eucharistic presence. Recent liturgical directives have explicitly acknowledged this principle and have extended this usage.[33]

(c) Lutherans traditionally have understood the Roman Catholic use of the term 'transubstantiation' to involve:

a. An emphatic affirmation of the presence of Christ's body and blood in the sacrament. With this they are in agreement.

b. An affirmation that God acts in the eucharist, effecting a change in the elements. This also Lutherans teach, although they use a different terminology.[34]

c. A rationalistic attempt to explain the mystery of Christ's presence in the sacrament. This they have rejected as presumptuous.

d. A definitive commitment to one and only one conceptual framework in which to express the change in the elements. This they have regarded as theologically untenable.

It can thus be seen that there is agreement on the 'that', the full reality of Christ's presence. What has been disputed is a particular way of stating the 'how', the manner in which he becomes present.

Today, however, when Lutheran theologians read contemporary Catholic expositions, [35] it becomes clear to them that the dogma of transubstantiation intends to affirm the fact of Christ's presence and of the change which takes place, and is not an attempt to explain how Christ becomes present. When the dogma is understood in this way, Lutherans find that they also must acknowledge that it is a legitimate way of attempting to express the mystery, even though they continue to believe that the conceptuality associated with 'transubstantiation' is misleading and therefore prefer to avoid the term.

Our conversations have persuaded us of both the legitimacy and the limits of theological efforts to explore the mystery of Christ's presence in the sacrament. We are also persuaded that no single vocabulary or conceptual framework can be adequate, exclusive, or final in this theological enterprise. We are convinced that current theological trends in both traditions give great promise for increasing convergence and deepened understanding of the eucharistic mystery.

CONCLUSION

There are still other questions that must be examined before we Catholic and Lutheran participants in these conversations would be prepared to assess our over-all agreements and disagreements on the doctrine of the sacrament of the altar. To mention two important omissions, we have not yet attempted to clarify our respective positions on the roles of the laity and the clergy, the 'general' and 'special' priesthood, in sacramental celebrations, nor have we discussed the pressing problem of the possibilities of intercommunion apart from full doctrinal and ecclesiastical fellowship.

On the two major issues which we have discussed at length, however, the progress has been immense. Despite all remaining differences in the ways we speak and think of the eucharistic sacrifice and our Lord's presence in his supper, we are no longer

43

ablet to regard ourselves as divided in the one holy catholic and apostolic faith on these two points. We therefore prayerfully ask our fellow Lutherans and Catholics to examine their consciences and root out many ways of thinking, speaking, and acting, both individually and as Churches, which have obscured their unity in Christ on these as on many other matters.

PARTICIPANTS
ROMAN CATHOLIC

The Most Revd T. Austin Murphy, Auxiliary Bishop of Baltimore, Maryland

The Revd Fr Thomas E. Ambrogi, SJ, Professor of Sacramental Theology and Ecumenics, Woodstock College, Woodstock, Maryland

The Very Revd Mgr Joseph W. Baker, Vice-Chairman of the Ecumenical Commission of the Archdiocese of St Louis, Missouri

The Very Revd Mgr William W. Baum, Chancellor of the Diocese of Kansas City-St Joseph, Missouri

The Revd Fr Raymond E. Brown, SS, Professor of Sacred Scripture, St Mary's Seminary, Baltimore, Maryland

The Revd Fr Walter Burghardt, SJ, Professor of Patristics, Woodstock College, Woodstock, Maryland

The Revd Fr Godfrey Diekmann, OSB, Professor of Patristics, St John's Abbey, Collegeville, Minnesota

The Revd Fr Maurice C. Duchaine, SS, Professor of Dogmatic Theology, St Mary's Seminary, Baltimore, Maryland

The Revd Fr John F. Hotchkin, Assistant Director, Bishops' Committee for Ecumenical and Interreligious Affairs, Washington, D.C.

Professor James F. McCue, School of Religion, University of Iowa, Iowa City, Iowa

The Revd Fr Harry J. McSorley, CSP, Professor of Ecumenical Theology, St Paul's College, Washington, D.C.

The Revd Fr Jerome D. Quinn, Professor of Old and New Testament, St Paul's Seminary, St Paul, Minnesota

The Revd Fr George Tavard, AA, Department of Religious Studies, Pennsylvania State University, University Park, Pennsylvania

LUTHERAN

Dr Paul C. Empie, General Secretary of the U.S.A. National Committee of the Lutheran World Federation, New York

Dr Arnold Carlson, Executive Secretary, Division of Theological Studies of the Lutheran Council in the U.S.A., New York

Dr Bertil E. Gartner, Professor of New Testament, Princeton Theological Seminary, Princeton, New Jersey

Dr Kent S. Knutson, Professor of Systematic Theology, Luther Theological Seminary, St Paul, Minnesota

Dr Fred Kramer, Professor of Dogmatics, Concordia Theological Seminary, Springfield, Illinois

Dr George Lindbeck, Associate Professor of Historical Theology, Yale University Divinity School, New Haven, Connecticut

Dr Paul Opsahl, Associate Executive Secretary, Division of Theological Studies of the Lutheran Council in the U.S.A., New York

Dr Arthur Carl Piepkorn, Graduate Professor of Systematic Theology, Concordia Seminary, St Louis, Missouri

Dr Warren Quanbeck, Professor of Systematic Theology, Luther Theological Seminary, St Paul, Minnesota

Dr John Reumann, Professor of New Testament at Lutheran Seminary, Philadelphia, Pennsylvania

Dr Joseph Sittler, Professor of Systematic Theology, University of Chicago Divinity School, Chicago, Illinois

Dr Krister Stendahl, Professor of Biblical Studies, Harvard University Divinity School, Cambridge, Massachusetts

NOTES

1. Various terms are current in the different Christian traditions for this sacrament: e.g., eucharist, holy communion, sacrament of the altar, mass. We shall use them interchangeably. Further, in order to mark the way our statement shares in the growing ecumenical consensus, we shall, on occasion, use language from the documents of the Ecumenical Movement to express our own convictions.

2. Scripture and the history of theology contain many ways of describing Christ's sacrifice and therefore also the sacrificial character of the memorial of that sacrifice which is the eucharist. The most general meaning of 'sacrifice' is broader than any current in contemporary usage—or in that of the sixteenth century. Thus, according to the Second World Conference on Faith and Order (Edinburgh 1937), 'If sacrifice is understood as it was by our Lord and his followers and in the early Church, it includes, not his death only, but the obedience of his earthly ministry, and his risen and ascended life, in which he still does his Father's

will and ever liveth to make intercession for us' (L. Vischer, ed., *A Documentary History of the Faith and Order Movement, 1927-1963* (St Louis 1963), p. 57). In what follows, however, no particular theory of 'sacrifice' or of related terms such as 'propitiation' is presupposed.

3. *Consultation on Church Union: Principles* (Cincinnati 1967), p. 50. See also the Montreal Faith and Order affirmation: the Lord's supper is 'a sacrament of the presence of the crucified and glorified Christ until he come, and a means whereby the sacrifice of the cross, which we proclaim, is operative within the church' (P. C. Rodger, ed., *The Fourth World Conference on Faith and Order: Montreal 1963*, p. 73).

4. Rodger, op. cit., pp. 73-4. See also the *Apology of the Augsburg Confession* xxiv, 30-88, esp. 33, 35, 74-5, 87. References to the Lutheran Confessions are based on *Die Bekenntnisschriften der Evangelisch-Lutherischen Kirche* (5th edn, Göttingen 1964).

5. Rodger, op. cit., p. 73

6. Luther says: 'not that we offer Christ as a sacrifice, but that Christ offers us'; but he also holds that this involves a sense in which 'we offer Christ': 'Through it [faith], in connection with the sacrament, we offer ourselves, our need, our prayer, praise, and thanksgiving in Christ, and thereby we offer Christ. . . . I also offer Christ in that I desire and believe that he accepts me and my prayer and praise and presents it to God in his own person' (*A Treatise on the New Testament,* in *Luther's Works* 35 (Philadelphia 1961) pp. 98-101). This agrees with the testimony of the Second Vatican Council, which, quoting St Augustine, says that the 'aim' of the sacrifice offered in the eucharist is that 'the entire commonwealth of the redeemed, that is, the community and the society of the saints, be offered as a universal sacrifice to God through the High Priest who in his Passion offered his very self for us that we might be the body of so exalted a Head' (*Decree on the Ministry and Life of Priests,* no. 2; E.T., W. M. Abbott and J. Gallagher, edd., *The Documents of Vatican II* (London and New York 1966) pp. 535-36; quotation from Augustine's *City of God* 10, 6). The continuation of this quotation is paraphrased in the 1947 encyclical *Mediator Dei,* no. 125: 'in the sacrament of the altar which she [the church] offers, she herself is also offered'. The contemporary Catholic theologian, Karl Rahner, explains this point by saying that the eucharistic offering of Christ inseparably involves 'the believing, inner "yes" of men to the movement of loving obedience of Christ to the Father'. He goes on to speak directly to the fears which Protestants have expressed regarding the notion of the 'sacrifice of the mass': 'The sacrifice of the mass creates no new gracious and saving will in God vis-à-vis the world which did not already exist through the cross (and only

46

through the cross!)'. 'We can speak of 'moving' God to forgiveness, reconciliation, mercy, and assistance through the sacrifice of the mass only in the sense that the gracious will of God, founded exclusively on the reconciliation of the cross, becomes visible in the sacrifice of the mass, comes to man . . . and takes hold of him' —producing, Rahner goes on to suggest, manifold effects in the worshippers and through their actions and prayers, in the world ('Die vielen Messen und das eine Opfer', in *Zeitschrift für katholische Theologie 71* (1949) pp. 267 and 268).

7. A question can stil be raised whether the word 'propitiatory', given its usual connotations, correctly describes the Father's action in Christ on Calvary. Cf. C. F. D. Moule, *The Sacrifice of Christ* (London 1956; Philadelphia 1964) pp. vi-viii, 33 f., and the literature cited on p . 46.

8. Denzinger-Schonmetzer 1753 (950)

9. XXXIV, 94

10. A. Vonier, *Collected Works 2* (London 1952), p. 343. It should be noted that Vonier does not regard such a statement as irreconciliable with his own insistence on the uniqueness and sufficiency of Christ's sacrifice.

11. Cf. *Constitution on the Sacred Liturgy*, nos. 26 and 27

12. Cf. *Constitution on the Sacred Liturgy*, no. 7; St Augustine, *Treatise on the Gospel of John 6, 1.7* (PL 35, 1428)

13. Cf. *Constitution on the Sacred Liturgy*, no. 7; *Instruction on Eucharistic Worship* (25 May 1967) no. 9; FC (=*Formula of Concord*) SD (=*Solid Declaration*) VIII, 76-84

14. 1 Cor. 11.27. Cf. Denzinger-Schonmetzer (hereafter DS) 1636, 1640 f., 1651, 1653. Writing of the eucharistic presence, E. Schlink states: 'The divine nature of Christ is not without the human nature and the human nature is not without the divine nature' (*Theology of the Lutheran Confessions* (Philadelphia 1961), p. 158). See also FC SD VII, 60; VIII, 76-84.

15. Cf. DS 1636; Ap (=*Apology of the Augsburg Confession*)x, 1, 4; FC Ep (=Epitome) VII, 6, 34; SD VII 88, 126

16. DS 1636. Cf. FC SD VII, 38

17. Cf. DS 1636; FC Ep VII, 16 f., SD VII, 97-103, 106

18. DS 1636. Cf. FC Ep VII, 15; SD VII 63

19. FC Ep VII, 14 f. In the context of the *Formula of Concord*, it is clear that 'spiritual' here is not opposed to 'real'. Cf. SD VII, 94-106, 108

20. Cf. AC (=*Augsburg Confession*) x; Ap x, 1 ff; FC Ep VII, 6 f., 26 ff., 34; SD VII, 2-11, 38, 48 f., DS 1636, 1651

21. Cf. DS 1651; FC SD VII, 7, 49, 116; *Constitution on the Sacred Liturgy*, nos. 33, 59; *Instruction on Eucharistic Worship*, no. 6

22. *Consultation on Church Union: Principles*, p. 49

23. Cf. LC (=*Large Catechism*) V, 9 f., 14; FC Ep VII, 9, 35; SD

47

VII, 73-82, 89, 121; DS 1636 f., 1640. See also DS 1612; FC Ep VII, 8; SD VII, 16, 32, 89; LC IV, 52, and V, 4 ff., 15-18. Catholics see in these affirmations of the Lutheran Confessions the essential content of the Catholic doctrine of the *exopere operato* working of the sacraments. In some of the pre-Tridentine Confessions, Lutherans rejected a concept of *opus operatum* which Catholics do not recognize as their own. Cf. DS 1606 ff., 1612.

24. Cf. AC X, 1; FC SD VII, 14; Ep VII, 6: 'We believe . . . that in the holy supper the body and blood of Christ are truly and essentially present and are truly distributed and received (*wahrhaftig ausgeteilet und empfangen werde*). . . .' In his *Sermon on the Sacrament of the Body and Blood of Christ* (1526; WA [=Weimar edition] 19, 491, 13), Luther declared: 'As soon as Christ says: "This is my body", his body is present through the Word and the power of the Holy Spirit' (E.T., F. Ahrens, American edition 36, 341). Cf. WA 30/1, 53, 122.—Trent (DS 1654) refers to Christ's presence before reception as 'ante [usum]'. For Trent *usus* means the actual reception by the communicant: 'in usu, dum sumitur' (ibid.). Lutherans speak of the whole liturgical action as *usus*: the consecration, distribution, and reception (*sumptio*) of the sacrament (FC SD VII, 85 f.). If, therefore, Lutherans do not speak of Christ being present before or apart from 'use', this is not to be understood as contradicting Trent; for the Lutheran Confessions agree that Jesus is present (*adesse*) in the sacrament before he is received (*sumi*), that is, *ante sumptionem*. It is 'the body and blood of Christ' which 'are distributed to us to eat and to drink. . . . (SD VII, 82).

25. DS 1643: '(sacramentum) quod fuerit a Christo Domino, ut sumatur, institutum'.

26. Cf. Phil. 2.10

27. Cf. DS 1643, 1656; FC SD VII, 126; one must not 'deny that Christ himself, true God and man, who is truly and essentially present in the Supper when it is rightly used, should be adored in spirit and in truth in all places, but especially where his community is assembled' (ed. T. G. Tappert). See also Luther, WA 11, 447 (Amer. edn 36, 194); St Augustine, *On Psalm 98*, 9 (PL 37, 1264).

28. *Instruction on Eucharistic Worship*, no. 49

29. Cf. Ibid. As Dom Lambert Beauduin has expressed it, the eucharist was not reserved in order to be adored; rather, because it was reserved, it was adored (cf. *Mélanges liturgiques . . . de Dom L. Beauduin* (Louvain 1954) p. 265). It should be noted, however, that adoration of the reserved sacrament has been very much a part of Catholic life and a meaningful form of devotion to Catholics for many centuries.

30. *Instruction on Eucharistic Worship,* no. 58; cf. *Constitution on the Sacred Liturgy,* no. 13
31. AC XXII, 1
32. Cf. *Constitution on the Sacred Liturgy,* no. 55. It should be noted that some scholars hold the communion under both kinds has not always been the practice within the church even in ancient times. For example, J. Jeremias (*The Eucharistic Words of Jesus* (New York 1964: London 1966), p. 115) suggest that 'the breaking of the bread' in the New Testament refers to communion under one species. Other scholars disagree.
33. Cf. *Instruction on Eucharistic Worship,* no. 32
34. Lutherans traditionally speak of the change that takes place in the elements as involving a sacramental union with the body and blood of Christ analogous to the hypostatic union of the human and divine natures in Christ; cf. FC SD VII, 36 f. Coupled with this affirmation is the statement that the bread and wine are essentially untransformed (*unvorwandelten*); cf. SD VII, 35 ff. In Ep VII, 22 the Roman Catholic affirmation of transubstantiation is understood to involve an annihilation (*zunicht werden*) of the bread and wine. It should be noted, however, that Trent's understanding of transubstantiation has nothing to do with the idea of annihilation of the elements. Catholic theologians emphasize today that the substantial change of bread and wine is a sacramental change which involves no change in 'the chemical, physical, or botanical reality of bread and wine' (E. Schillebeeckx, 'Transubstantiation, Transfinalization, Transignification', in *Worship* 40 (1966) 337). Further, on the basis of Ap X, 2, which cites with approval the Greek tradition that the bread is truly changed into the body of Christ ('mutato pane'; 'panem . . . vere mutari'), there is a certain sense in which 'one can stand on Lutheran ground and talk about a transformation of the elements (*Verwandlung der Elemente*)'. Cf. Fr Brunstaed, *Theologie der lutherischen Bekenntnisschriften* (Gutersloh 1951), p. 156.
35. Cf. K. Rahner, 'The Presence of Christ in the Sacrament of the Lord's Supper', in *Theological Investigations* 4 (London and Baltimore 1966), pp. 287-311; E. Schillebeeckx, 'Christus tegenwoordigheid in de Eucharistie', in *Tijdschrift voor Theologie* 5 (1965), pp. 136-72.

Group of Les Dombes

TOWARDS A COMMON EUCHARISTIC FAITH

*Agreement between
Roman Catholics and
Protestants*

TRANSLATED BY
Pamela Gaughan

First published 1972
in French with the title Vers une même foi eucharistique?
by Les Presses de Taizé, 71460 Taizé-Communauté, France
©   Groupe des Dombes 1972

©   Translation, S.P.C.K. 1973

INTRODUCTION

The agreement on the eucharist which is the subject of this little book is the fruit of many years of work on the part of the inter-confessional Group of Les Dombes, so that, to understand it properly, it is important to situate it in the context in which it was drawn up and to circumscribe it accurately.

The Group was founded in 1937 by the Abbé Paul Couturier of Lyons, promoter of the Week of Prayer for Christian Unity. The success of the formula this great spiritual leader proposed to all Christians in 1935 is well known. He invited them to pray together 'for the Unity that Christ wills, by the means he wills' and for 'the sanctification of all, whatever their confession'. In the space of a few months this appeal gained the support of considerable sections of the Orthodox, Anglican, and French Protestant Churches (Synod of Agen 1936) and was soon to achieve worldwide acceptance for the Week of Prayer. Gradually a climate of fraternity and love was built up—it has been hailed as a Copernican revolution—which was to enable the Roman Catholic Church, at the Second Vatican Council, to join *officially* in the Ecumenical Movement (Decree *Unitatis Redintegratio* of 21 November 1964). It was only then that dialogues on an equal footing could be instituted between the Vatican and the non-Roman Catholic Churches and communities.

Paul Couturier died on 24 March 1953, having seen only the first stages of the new trend. But, as soon as he had secured the support of the Synod of Agen for his proposal of universal prayer, he had sought to form a doctrinal working group of Catholic priests and Protestant pastors at the Trappist monas-tery of Les Dombes (Ain), whose Abbot offered him a hospit-able refuge as discreet as it was fraternal. Thus was planted the seed of a modest institution which grew steadily and flourished until today, thirty-five years afterwards, it is more vigorous than ever.

The founder of the Group imbued the talks at Les Dombes

with a profound and unerring spirituality, centred on the priestly prayer of Christ (John 17), an evangelical prayer which has indeed now become the ecumenical prayer. He impregnated us with it, literally. 'Let each one of us', he liked to say, 'allow Christ to pray in him his prayer of unity for our brothers of the other Churches', and this reciprocity brought about a perfect limpidity in our relations. It is important to bear witness to the fact that this strong spiritual drive persists, both in our Group and among the monks whose silent company enfolds us. The doctrinal path traced at Les Dombes has been described more than once;[1] it is enough here to recall its general lines (and its continuity) in order to bring out clearly the deep roots of the texts we are presenting here.

From the start the Abbé Couturier sought to guide the Group's discussions towards an ecumenical theology to which all the participants would set their seal and in this he stood out as a forerunner. His intuition concerning the 'complementarity' of points of Catholic and Reformed doctrine—when each was shorn of its polemical features—was surprising in a man who was not a theologian by profession; he instinctively glimpsed the level of the 'super-problems' where, rising above traditional controversies, a higher synthesis could begin to emerge. This was the fruit of his contemplation, for he lived constantly steeped in the mystery of God. In his eyes all theology ought to be spiritual —*theologia sacra*. And so it was that, with his customary discretion, he enlightened with his counsel the theologians he gathered around him and opened up new avenues for their reflection. The future was to show that he was right.

But it was only by degrees that this goal could be reached. The members of the Group needed first to know one another thoroughly, thanks to talks about broad subjects selected somewhat at random. This was the phase of Christian brotherhood, which created a climate of mutual trust among the initial participants. There followed a period of comparative theology centred on such themes as tradition, Scripture, the sacraments. Practice perfected a rigorous method of approach: each subject was circumscribed in depth, placed in its right perspective, and reduced to its proper proportions—a thing unknown in classical theology—and little by little, lines of convergence emerged. In 1956 the idea took root of formulating 'theses' and we persisted in it. In 1963, when we decided to take stock of what had been achieved to date, we had a number of important agreements behind us: in Christian anthropology, Christology, ecclesiology, Pneumatology, eschatology. They were recorded, with commentaries, in No. 70 of *Verbum Caro* and reproduced in the Taizé Press booklet, *Dialogue oecuménique*. By this time our work, discreet though it sought to be, was already known to the World Council of Churches at Geneva (Faith and Order Commission) as well as to the Roman Secretariat for Unity, by the intermediary of those of us who belonged to one or other of those bodies. Henceforth it was to receive a certain amount of attention as well as encouragement, thanks to the appearance of the Vatican Council's Decree *Unitatis Redintegratio* (1964). Were not our theses an illustration, in anticipation, of the possibilities latent in that Decree?

A new stage began in 1964. Our team was reinforced by a number of valuable members: Jean Bosc, professor at the Faculty of Protestant Theology of the University of Paris, followed by Paul Evdokimov of the Institut Saint Serge—the first a great scholar of Calvin, whom he read in an ecumenical spirit, the second nurtured by the Early Fathers and both of them men of true spirituality. Paul Evdokimov, it should be noted, did not confront us as the Orthodox corner of the triangle; he was a lucid observer, always ready to help us overcome the conflicts of the West from which the East had not suffered.

With them we took up again the study of two major themes: the Holy Spirit (in itself, in the Church, and in Christian life) and the eucharist, with the ambition here of ridding this dogma of all the controversy that had built up around it since the Reformation. In fact we had already been prepared for this by much persevering work of 'Christological concentration' and our ideas converged on certain outstanding points: *The Church as the Body of Christ* (1958), *The Authority and Presidential Role of the Ministry* (1959), *The Apostolic Succession* (1960), *Ministerial Priesthood in relation to Universal Priesthood* (1962). On the other hand, the first mutterings of the post-Conciliar crisis were beginning to make themselves heard and the problem of intercommunion was thrust to the fore and fomented by all sorts of abuses, in the midst of which ecumenism was in danger of being carried away and lost to sight. This distressing situation stimulated us and we felt ourselves committed to working, no longer opposite one another, but side by side, in an endeavour to formulate a common creed where the eucharist was concerned.

The texts reproduced below are the fruit of these latter years of effort. There are two of them—in the first place a doctrinal text, far the more important of the two. It evades none of the traditional difficulties and in regard to each of them achieves substantial agreement, subject to certain 'clarifications' that are clearly indicated. It is strictly confined to eucharistic doctrine, the problem of the mutual recognition of our respective ministries being left to subsequent research.

The second text, pastoral in character, has a different origin. It was built up on an outline provided on request by a number of chaplains of schools and youth movements, Roman Catholic priests, and Protestant pastors. The outline was discussed at Les Dombes and subsequently amended by an exchange of correspondence and drafted in everyday language. It is reproduced here simply as a draft text and *must be read as a prolongation of the preceding one*. Both texts are accompanied by commentaries which clarify all the doubtful points.

By the juxtaposition of these two texts the Group seeks to show that it is not an academic body. We always have our ear to the needs of the Church and desire to place ourselves at the service of all Christian people.

DOCTRINAL AGREEMENT ON THE EUCHARIST

1. Today, when Christians celebrate the eucharist and proclaim the gospel, they feel themselves increasingly to be brothers in the midst of their fellow-men, with a mission and an eagerness to bear witness together to the same Christ, by word and deed and by their eucharistic celebration. That is why, for some years past, the Group meeting at Les Dombes has been scrutinizing the significance of mutual eucharistic hospitality and joint celebration and the conditions on which they depend.

2. One particularly important condition of this sharing of the Lord'st table is substantial agreement on what it is, despite theological diversities.

3. The Group takes over the text of the Faith and Order agreement (1968) (on pp. 79-89 of this book), seeking to clarify, adapt, and amplify it in the light of the interconfessional situation in France today.

I THE EUCHARIST: THE LORD'S SUPPER

4. The eucharist is the sacramental meal, the new paschal meal of God's people, which Christ, having loved his disciples unto the end, gave them before his death that they might celebrate it in the light of the resurrection until his coming.

5. This meal is the effective sign of the gift that Christ made of himself as the bread of life, through the sacrifice of his life and his death and by his resurrection.

6. In the eucharist, Christ fulfils in a surpassing manner his promise to be amongst those who gather together in his name.

II THE EUCHARIST: ACT OF THANKSGIVING TO THE FATHER

7. The eucharist is the great act of thanksgiving to the Father

for all that he has accomplished in the creation and redemption of the world, for all that he is now accomplishing in the Church and in the world, despite man's sin, and for all that he is seeking to accomplish through the coming of his Kingdom. Thus, the eucharist is the blessing (*berakah*) whereby the Church expresses gratitude to God for all his benefits.

8. The eucharist is the great sacrifice of praise in which the Church speaks in the name of all creation. For the world which God reconciled with himself in Christ is present at each eucharist: in the bread and the wine, in the persons of the faithful and in the prayers they offer for all mankind. Thus the eucharist opens up to the world the way to its transfiguration.

III THE EUCHARIST: MEMORIAL OF CHRIST

9. Christ instituted the eucharist as a memorial (*anamnesis*) of his whole life and above all of his cross and resurrection. Christ, with everything he has accomplished for us and for all creation, is present himself in this memorial, which is also a foretaste of his Kingdom. The memorial, in which Christ acts through the joyful celebration of his Church, implies this re-presentation and this anticipation. Therefore it is not only a matter of recalling to mind a past event or even its significance. The memorial is the effective proclamation by the Church of the great work of God. By its communion with Christ, the Church participates in this reality from which it draws its life.

10. The memorial, being at once re-presentation and anticipation, is lived out in thanksgiving and intercession. Making the memorial of the passion, resurrection, and ascension of Christ, our High Priest and Mediator, the Church presents to the Father the one perfect sacrifice of his Son and asks him to accord every man the benefit of the great work of redemption it proclaims.

11. Thus, united to our Lord, who offers himself to his Father, and in communion with the universal Church in heaven and on earth, we are renewed in the covenant sealed with the blood of Christ and we offer ourselves as a living and holy sacrifice which must be expressed in the whole of our daily life.

12. The memorial of Christ is the essential content of the Word proclaimed, as it is of the eucharist. The celebration of the eucharist and the proclamation of the Word go hand in hand, for the ministry of the Word is directed towards the eucharist and the eucharist in turn implies and fulfils the Word.

IV The Eucharist: Gift of the Spirit

13. The memorial, in the deep sense that we have given to it, implies the invocation of the Spirit (*epiclesis*). Christ, in his heavenly intercession, asks the Father to send his Spirit to his children. And so the Church, living in the new covenant, prays with confidence for the Spirit, in order to be renewed and sanctified by the bread of life, led in truth and strengthened to fulfil its mission in the world.

14. It is the Spirit which, invoked over the congregation, over the bread and wine, makes Christ really present to us, gives him to us and enables us to perceive him. The memorial and the invocation of the Spirit (*anamnesis* and *epiclesis*), directed towards our union with Christ, cannot be accomplished independently of the communion.

15. The gift of the Holy Spirit in the eucharist is a foretaste of the kingdom of God: the Church receives the life of the new creation and the assurance of our Lord's return.

16. We recognize that the eucharistic prayer as a whole has the character of an *epiclesis*.

V The Sacramental Presence of Christ

17. The act of the eucharist is the gift of Christ's person. The Lord said: 'Take, eat, this is my body which is given for you.' 'Drink ye all of this, for this is my blood of the new covenant which is shed for you and for many for the remission of sins.' We accordingly confess unanimously the real, living, and effective presence of Christ in this sacrament.

18. To discern the body and blood of Christ requires faith. However, the presence of Christ revealed to his Church in the

eucharist does not depend on the faith of the individual, for it is Christ who binds himself in his words and in the Spirit to the sacramental act, the sign of his presence given.

19. Christ's act being the gift of his body and blood, that is to say of himself, the reality given in the signs of the bread and wine is his body and his blood.[2] It is by virtue of Christ's creative word and by the power of the Holy Spirit that the bread and wine are made a sacrament and hence a 'sharing of the body and blood of Christ' (1 Cor. 10.16). They are henceforth, in their ultimate truth, beneath the outward sign, the given reality, and so they remain, since their purpose is to be consumed. What is given as the body and blood of Christ remains given as his body and blood and requires to be treated as such.

20. Noting the diversity of practice among Christian denominations[3] and at the same time drawing from the preceding agreement the necessary conclusions regarding the change of heart (*metanoia*) on the part of the Churches that is seen to be essential, we ask that:

i. On the Roman Catholic side it be pointed out, in particular by catechists and preachers, that the primary purpose of reserving the eucharist is for its distribution to the sick and the absent;[4]

ii. On the Protestant side the best means should be adopted of showing the respect due to the elements that have served for the celebration of the eucharist, which is to consume them subsequently, without precluding their use for the communion of the sick.

VI THE EUCHARIST: COMMUNION IN THE BODY OF CHRIST

21. By giving himself to the communicants, Christ unites them in his body. It is in this sense that one can say: if the Church makes the eucharist, the eucharist makes the Church. The sharing of the one bread and the one cup in a given place makes the communicants one with the whole Christ, with one another, and with all other communicants at all times and in all places. By sharing the one bread they manifest their member-

ship of the Church in its universality, the mystery of the redemption is revealed to their eyes, and the whole body grows in grace. The communion is thus the source and strength of all community life among Christians.

22. By his cross, Christ has broken down all the barriers that separate men. We cannot communicate with him in truth, therefore, unless we labour, in the midst of the conflict in which we are involved, to do away with the barriers in the Church that separate races, nationalities, languages, classes, denominations.

23. According to Christ's promise, every believer and member of his body receives in the eucharist the remission of his sins and everlasting life and is fed with the food of faith, hope, and love.

24. Fellowship in the eucharistic communion in the body of Christ (*agape*) and the attentions that Christians have for one another and for the world should find a means of expression in the liturgy: by the mutual forgiveness of sins, the kiss of peace, the offering of gifts to be used for community meals or for distribution to brothers in need, the brotherly welcome extended to all regardless of political, social, or cultural differences.

VII THE EUCHARIST: A MISSION IN THE WORLD

25. The mission of the Church does not simply stem from the eucharist. Whenever the Church is really the Church, its mission is part of its life. In the eucharist the Church is fully itself and is united with Christ in his mission.

26. The world is already present in the act of thanksgiving to the Father, in which the Church speaks in the name of all creation; in the memorial where, united with Christ the Redeemer and Mediator, the Church prays for the world: in the invocation of the Spirit, in which it hopes for sanctification and the new creation.

27. Reconciled in the eucharist, the members of the body of Christ become the servants of reconciliation among men and witnesses of the joy of the resurrection. Their presence in the world implies fellowship in suffering and hope with all men,

among whom they are called upon to bear witness to the love of Christ in service and in combat. The celebration of the eucharist, the breaking of a bread that is necessary to life, is an incitement not to accept conditions in which men are deprived of bread, justice, and peace.

28. The eucharist is also the feast of the perpetual apostolic harvest, in which the Church rejoices for the gifts received in the world.

VIII THE EUCHARIST: BANQUET OF THE KINGDOM[5]

29. Our Lord instituted the eucharist for the time from his ascension until his coming again. This is the time of hope and that is why the eucharist directs our thoughts to the Lord's coming and brings it near to us. It is a joyful anticipation of the heavenly banquet, when redemption shall be fully accomplished and all creation shall be delivered from bondage.

30. Thus, by giving the eucharist to his Church, which, in its weakness, will live to the last in the midst of suffering and strife, our Lord enables it to take new heart and to persevere.

31. This Church that Christ feeds throughout its pilgrimage perceives, above and beyond the divisions that still persist, that the eschatological meeting-place is an ecumenical meeting-place, where Israel and all the nations will be gathered together into one people.

IX THE PRESIDENCY OF THE EUCHARIST

32. Christ, in the eucharist, gathers together and feeds his Church at a meal over which he presides.

33. The sign of Christ's presidency is given in the presiding minister, whom he has called and sent. The mission of ministers has its roots in and is modelled on that of the apostles, which is transmitted to the Church by the imposition of hands accompanied by the invocation of the Holy Spirit. This transmission implies the continuity of the ministry, fidelity to apostolic teaching, and a life lived according to the gospel.[6]

34. The minister shows that the congregation is not proprietor of the action it is performing, that it is not the master of the eucharist but receives it from Another, Christ living in his Church. While remaining a member of the congregation, the minister is at the same time the man sent to signify God's action and the link between the local community and the other communities in the universal Church.

35. In their mutual relations, the eucharistic gathering and its president live their dependence on the one Lord and great High Priest. In its relation to the minister, the congregation is exercising its royal priesthood conferred on it by Christ, the priest. In his relation to the congregation, the minister is living his presidency as the servant of Christ, the pastor.

X CONCLUSION

36. At this stage in our quest we give thanks that the major difficulties concerning the eucharistic faith have been removed.

37. We realize, however, that some clarification is still required in regard to the permanence of the sacramental presence and the precise place of the apostolic succession in the ministry. It seems to us that any joint participation in the eucharist demands a real effort to overcome these difficulties and, if need be, on both sides, the abandonment of everything that is marked by controversy within our various denominational positions.

38. The pursuance of our quest is bound to enrich us still further with the complementary spiritual values among which we live. We can never exhaust the understanding of a mystery which is beyond all understanding and calls us unceasingly to come out of ourselves in order to live in thanksgiving and wonder at this supreme gift of Christ to his Church.

XI RECOMMENDATION

39. It is often asked today what degree of concordance of belief is required for a Christian to be received by another Church at its communion table. Without claiming to solve here the other questions raised by the different cases of eucharistic hospitality,

we think that access to communion should not be refused for reasons of eucharistic belief to Christians of another denomination whose own faith is that professed above.[7]

40. That is why we ask the authorities of our respective Churches to consider carefully the new situation created by this agreement on the eucharist when they are weighing up the requests for hospitality addressed to them.

PASTORAL AGREEMENT
The Meaning of the Eucharist

I THE EUCHARIST: THE LORD'S SUPPER

Jesus, on the eve of his death, at a meal he was sharing with his disciples, took the bread and, having said grace, broke it and distributed it among them, saying: 'Take, eat, this is my body which is given for you. Do this in remembrance of me.' Then, taking a cup of wine, he gave thanks and passed it around, saying: 'Drink ye all of this, for this is my blood of the new covenant which is shed for you and for many for the remission of sins. Do this in remembrance of me.'

With these words he invited his disciples to repeat his action and Christians to respond to that invitation by coming together to celebrate the eucharist.

II MEETING WITH CHRIST IN HIS DEATH AND RESURRECTION

It is around Christ that we gather to meet him. He makes us live again his death and resurrection in the hope of his coming again, in joy and thankfulness to God. In this way the decisive events whereby we are reconciled with God and with one another are made present and real to us, although they are not repeated. Christ, who prays to his Father and offers himself up for all men, embraces us in his offering and commits us to the love and service of our brothers.

III THE REALITY OF CHRIST'S PRESENCE IN THE SACRAMENT

By sharing and consuming the bread and wine of the eucharist, we receive, according to the life-giving Word of the Lord, his body that is given, his blood that is shed, his whole person. This bread and this wine are thus the body and blood of Christ, given by him to his Church.

Fed, all of us, by Christ, who welcomes us to his table, we share his life as the Son of God and the brother of all mankind.

This life that we received at our baptism, the eucharist feeds and tends in its growth and prepares for its fulfilment in our resurrection.

IV INVOCATION AND ACTION OF THE SPIRIT

We celebrate the eucharist in the Holy Spirit, the light, love, and strength of God in the hearts of men. By it we move forward, from the coming of Jesus Christ among us until his last coming, towards the freedom and glory to which God calls us. This movement is going on in the Church today, thanks to the eucharist.

In the eucharistic prayer the Church asks for the promised coming of the Holy Spirit in order to receive and discern the presence of our Lord and to draw life from his death and resurrection.

V THE MINISTER OF THE EUCHARIST

As Christ once chose the apostles, so today he still chooses ministers to gather his Church together in prayer and to guide it in its mission.

The presence of one of these ministers, the servant of the Word and of the Sacrament, in the midst of the eucharistic gathering, means that Christ himself is presiding at the meal where he gives his body to be eaten.

This service of presiding also expresses the communion which our Lord creates between all the members of the congregation and between the individual local Churches in the bosom of the universal Church.

VI THE EUCHARIST: A FORCE FOR THE LIBERATION OF MANKIND

By the action of the Spirit and the ministry of the Church, Christ carries on the work for which he died and rose again: the work of freeing and reconciling all creation, in the first place by revealing to man the true face of God. When we accept his invitation to his table, we are taking up his mission in his footsteps by our witness of faith and hope, by our fight against the forces of oppression, destruction, and death, in order to reconcile all things and offer everything to God.

Communicating in the sacrament with the life, the death and the victory of Jesus, we must also live that communion in our daily lives in society, by our options and our actions, in the face of suffering and failure. We cannot allow conditions to endure in which millions of men are deprived of bread, justice, and peace.

VII THE EUCHARIST: SOURCE OF UNITY

Since they commit themselves jointly to uniting and freeing mankind, Christians are called upon to live with one another, in full communion, in the one Lord. In the state of separation in which they still find themselves, the eucharist underlines the scandal of their confessional differences and at the same time their inability to overcome them of their own accord.

But when Christ gives himself to us in the eucharist, he is leading us towards union, in his body, with all communicants at all times and in all places. Thereby he revives our hope of reaching it and strengthens our will to strive for it.

As Christ intended it, the gift of the eucharist overrides our divisions, not by denying or concealing them, but by giving us today the pledge and effective sign of the unity he is always asking of his Father: 'May they all be one . . . so that the world may believe' (Jerusalem Bible).

We hope that we have given expression to the content of Scripture and the traditional faith of the Church. We thank God who has enabled us to confess this faith together and we pray that he may hasten the day when we shall receive at the same table the body and blood of his Son.

COMMENTARY

The foregoing texts call for a certain number of explanations. It is important to know their basic intention, the circumstances and manner in which they were drafted, to whom precisely they are addressed and what are the most important points recommending them to the reader's attention.

1 THE BASIC INTENTION

These two texts, distinct in form but inseparable in substance, are the fruit of a number of years of work by the Group meeting at Les Dombes. The 'theses', drawn up from 1965, and especially from 1967, onwards, show fairly clearly the direction the work was taking and the stages through which it passed. On the basis of the dogma of the Trinity, 'whose mystery is revealed in the economy of salvation according to the Sciptures' (1965), we have sought to discern the deep meaning of the relation of the Church to Jesus Christ and to the Holy Spirit. In so doing we have become conscious of the central place of the eucharist in the life of the Church and we have been made attentive in consequence to the questions raised in our still separate Churches by the aspiration to be found increasingly among Christian people today towards 'intercommunion'.

That is accordingly the context of our doctrinal thinking as members of a team, while our pastoral endeavour has been directed towards serving our respective Churches in their quest for unity. It is in this context that what we have called 'a doctrinal agreement as to what is essential' with regard to the meaning of the eucharist and its significance for the Church is to be seen and understood.

We have not sought to evade any of the difficulties of dogma or ecclesiology; we have not sought either to overcome them entirely, but simply to seek a new approach and point out possible means of overcoming them, which it will be for our Churches themselves to judge and further by joint endeavour. We know, indeed, that the work is under way and the movement is growing at all levels throughout the world, as the many published documents and declarations, as well as more voluminous works, bear witness. And so we are simply contributing one more item to an already large dossier of documents, on more than one of which, moreover, we ourselves have drawn.[8]

2 METHOD OF WORK

Having regard to the agreements already recorded in our earlier theses, we adopted a method combining collective effort with synthesis. Taking as a starting-point the text of the 1968 *Ecumenical Agreement on the Eucharist* (Faith and Order), a small working party drew up the preparatory doctrinal document and sent it to all participants some months in advance. This first text was also submitted to a number of theologians outside the Group for their criticism. At a plenary session (September 1971) these comments were received and used, together with numerous amendments and partial rewordings proposed by the members present. This collective work culminated in a final text which enabled unanimous agreement to be reached at a second reading. The 'pastoral' text was read critically only once in plenary session. It was drawn up in its present form by a team which redrafted it in the light of the amendments proposed in writing and adopted by correspondence among the members of the Group.

3 WHAT DO WE MEAN BY AN 'AGREEMENT AS TO WHAT IS ESSENTIAL'?

Through centuries of controversy the divisions between our Churches have been aggravated by and drawn justification from disagreement on points of dogma which, precisely, one side or the other held to be essential, with the resulting subtraction of communion. Real unity of the Churches can accordingly be sought only on the basis of a common eucharistic faith considered sufficient to restore communion.

We could therefore neither be satisfied with a 'minimum' *beyond* which these disagreements would reappear, nor aim at a 'maximum' *this side of* which those same disagreements would merely be passed over in silence. It is clearly unthinkable that a common confession of eucharistic faith should result either from a 'subtraction' brought about by mutual concessions or from the 'addition' of a number of heterogeneous or conflicting statements of doctrine. *An agreement as to what is essential can only be reached in and through what is essential, namely Jesus Christ revealing and communicating himself to his Church in the unity of the Holy Spirit.*

As we wrote early in 1967, 'the attitude which consists in submitting the gift of faith to the scrutiny of the substance of the gospel, in a living relationship to the person of Christ by the action of the Spirit, has thrown new light on our respective positions and we must persevere in it'.[9] This we have endeavoured to do, seeking less to say what we regard as essential than to confess together with gratitude the essential thing that he, Christ, gives us by making us share in his being and his life in the sacramental mystery of the Church. To speak of the 'substance of the gospel' in relation to the mystery of the eucharist is to affirm that the person and work of Christ Jesus, which are the whole content of the gospel, are also the living and dynamic core of the eucharist. To speak of a 'new light' being thrown on our respective positions is to believe in the enlightening and unifying power of the Holy Spirit which, by purifying them and freeing them from the inflexibility of polemics, clarifies them and restores them to their original intention of profound fidelity to the truth of the mystery of Christ. We have not sought to challenge any particular formulation of dogma, still less to propose any new ones; by a process of questioning one another we have tried to examine our respective positions *in relation to what is essential,* not in order to abandon them but in order better to discern their real substance and hence their necessary reconciliation.

Thanks to this we have been enabled to take stock of what we have called the *metanoia* of the Churches, or 'confessional change of heart'. This is for us, Catholics and Protestants, a step that is at once difficult, demanding and hazardous:

Difficult, because it goes against our natural tendency to defend and justify our own Church in any doctrinal discussion;

Demanding, because it it called for by the Holy Spirit and at the same time in full solidarity with our respective Churches;

Hazardous, lastly, like every act of faith, which can never escape the snares of the Devil, who is always clever at distorting into more or less masochistic and sterile self-criticism what needs to remain a vigilant combat fought in faith and a plea for mercy fraught with hope.

That is the spirit in which we have endeavoured to work.

4 To whom is our Declaration addressed?

We addressed the doctrinal agreement in the first place (in September 1971) to *the authorities responsible for our Churches in France* (Episcopal Conference, National or Governing Council of the Reformed Church, and the Lutheran Church), not that the Group had in any way been acting under instructions from them, but we thought that while theological research demands freedom, it ought certainly not to be pursued on questions involving the faith of our Churches without them being called upon to think about the issues and consult together at the highest level. Our purpose is simply to supply food for such thought and a contribution to such mutual consultation, which we should like to see thorough enough to produce decisions.

It is for this reason too that we are publishing and circulating today this dossier addressed to *all Christian people*. By that we mean note only the people of our parishes but also the various groups and teams engaged in ecumenical research or action and all those who are looking for new forms of communion and witness for the service of the gospel among mankind today.

An agreement worked out and adopted by a group as small as ours cannot be expected to win the approval of all, in particular of those who have not followed our progress. It should produce reactions, debate, more searching enquiry. It can and must, we believe, help to stimulate an awareness of certain matters of urgency. One of the most pressing is the urgency of at last doing away with the many factors of segregation that exists today between theologians on the one hand and bishops and ministers on the other, between clergy and laymen, between 'traditionalists' and 'fringe-members'. There are at present in our parishes, our ecumenical groups, our movements, our 'mixed marriage' clubs, many Christians, sincere and adult, aware enough, if only because of their bitter experience of denominational stumbling-blocks set in the way of the full communion of the Churches, to be associated constructively with the quest for a common eucharistic faith otherwise than by exhortations to patience and repeatedly disappointed hopes. It is they, indeed, who are the communicants of our Churches and the Holy Spirit is at work in them just as it is in the hearts and consciences of the doctors and leaders.

And so it is with the hope of bringing about a concerted attitude, a mutual receptivity at all levels, that we have worked to the end that, in accordance with the gospel and with the help of the Holy Spirit, a 'consensus' may gradually form and 'con-

71

cord' (in the deepest sense), which is the fruit of the real, living, and active presence of Christ in his Church and which partakes of the nature of a 'mystery', may germinate and grow. That, let it be added, is the primary condition for the unhampered and unequivocal emergence, in a legitimate diversity of forms, of the one true dogma signified to us in the mystery itself.

It is accordingly for our Churches—leaders and members alike—to say whether our documents fulfil these requirements and hopes.

5 SOME DECISIVE POINTS

It is obvious that special attention will be paid to the passages of the doctrinal text where our agreement bears on points that, traditionally, have been the subject of controversy. For this reason we wish to explain their meaning and import.

1.   In the first place, the first three paragraphs form a whole and underline the three inseparable aspects of the eucharist. It is at once: the Lord's supper, a thanksgiving to the Father for the salvation of the whole world (eucharist in the strict sense) and the memorial (*anamnesis*) of the redemptive act of Christ, seen in its totality.

In this way, three features of the celebration of the eucharist are stated as dogma and restored to a balance that is often neglected in practice. They are:

(a) The specifically ecclesial character of the Lord's supper (too often considered from the angle of the individual). The Lord's supper is 'the new paschal meal of God's people', in which our Lord himself establishes his Church in a new and special relationship to himself (see part. VI).

(b) The act of thanksgiving to God for the *universal* redemption of the world accomplished in Jesus Christ. The world is present at each celebration. The eucharist is not simply a means of edification 'for internal use'; it is inseparable from the proclamation to the world of the 'Good News' of its reconciliation with God (this aspect is developed in VII, with the consequences it implies).

(c) Lastly and above all, the deep meaning and dynamic import of the *memorial*. It is not simply the commemoration of a past event, nor a repetition of the one sacrifice on the cross but, according to the biblical usage of the word *anamnesis*, it is at once the realization of the new covenant and the anticipation of its fulfilment in the person of him 'who is, who was, and who is to be'. If the act of redemption by the cross is at the centre of the great work of God, the memorial in the eucharist is not directed solely towards its sacrificial aspect but towards all its interdependent features: the life, death, resurrection, ascension, and last coming of Christ. That is why we speak of the 'memorial of Christ', whose sacrifice is the central event.

Thus the eucharist is not only the *act of the Church* assembled to offer its sacrifice of praise but at the same time an *act on the part of our Lord himself*, whereby he makes himself present to the Church he has redeemed by his own offering of himself.

2. *Hence the importance of the epiclesis (cf. iv above)*. The invocation of the Holy Spirit in the celebration of the eucharist is no pious formality but the very condition of the efficacity of this twofold action by our Lord and the Church. The promise and gift of the Holy Spirit are indeed the mark and the 'seal' of the new covenant. It is in and through the Holy Spirit that the congregation called together by Christ to eat and drink the bread and wine enter into real communion with him, perceiving and receiving in reality his body and his blood. Just as one cannot dissociate the sign from the reality, neither can one dissociate the *epiclesis* upon the congregation: ('send down upon us thy Holy Spirit' from the *epiclesis* upon the visible signs 'this bread and this wine'), for it is by the same Spirit that the people gathered together communicate with Christ by feeding on his body and his blood in the species of bread and wine.

3. Thus our joint affirmation of the *real presence* of Christ (cf. v above) is not founded on an abstract definition of the sacrament but on the word of the Lord himself, which we believe not only *states* but also *creates* (cf. Ps. 33.9: 'He spoke and it was created; he commanded and there it stood' (Jerusalem Bible)).

It is this biblical realism that enables us better to place in its setting the Word—Faith—Sacrament relationship, leaving aside both the spiritualistic subjectivism that makes Christ's presence depend on the faith of the communicants (and, taken to the extreme, reduces the sign to nothing) and the materialism which sees in the things themselves—the species—the more or less magical presence of Christ.

4. This approach to the mystery of the eucharist has accordingly enabled us to confront the particularly controversial issue of the *permanence of the presence*. What we found ourselves able to say, not without difficulty (paragraph 19 of section v above), may well appear to many Protestants to go too far and to many Roman Catholics not to go far enough, despite the references to St Thomas and Calvin in the footnote! That is why, on this specific point, we have ventured to recall the need for a 'change of heart' on the part of the Churches (as much as regards usage as in outlook), having regard to the many different practices, whose significance must be brought to light and which call for essential clarifications.

5. Nor did we seek to evade the thorny problem of the ministry, although confining ourselves to the minister's *presidential function at the eucharist*. How could we go further at a time when doctrinal research and practice are raising so many questions concerning the nature and specific mission of the priesthood and the ministry in our respective Churches? We have sought essentially to situate the role of the presiding minister in relation to the sacerdotal ministry of the Church, as God's people assembled with a mission to fulfil, and in relation to the ministry of Christ, the One, Universal, Pastor-Priest, whose presence must be 'signified' as service.

And so it is necessary to read this paragraph in the perspective of our earlier study of the apostolic succession (1968 theses) and of that carried out in 1968 and 1969 on the reconciliation of ministries. More clarification is still required, particularly in regard to the sacerdotal and sacramental character of ordination.[10] But here we feel that we have come to a substantial and sufficient doctrinal agreement on the subject of the presiding minister.[11] Again, theological research has to go hand in hand with the life of faith, witness, and service lived in common, which is something that is happening more and more.

Lastly, let it be said that, while we think it is necessary, for various reasons, to proceed by stages in our progress towards the unity of our Churches and hence of the eucharist, we believe just as much in the urgency of speeding the process up, precisely because of the urgency of the present mission of the Church. It is not by chance that what is said in our Declaration of 'solidarity in the eucharistic communion' relates directly to the mission of God's people in the world and precedes what is said about the special ministry which must necessarily be instituted to that end.

We hope that these few remarks will have given a sufficient indication of the scope and limits of our undertaking. In informing the authorities of our own Churches and all those who nourish ecumenical hopes of the point we have reached, it is with the intention of sharing with them the grace we have received, of strengthening the communion that already unites us and of 'giving way to one another in obedience to Christ' (Eph. 5.21, Jerusalem Bible).

CONCLUSION

Having reached the end of this little book, let us try to situate it in the present life of the Church in France. In the first place it bears witness to the cross-fertilization between theological research and the expression of the desires of many Christian communities. The headway being made by ecumenical groups of very different kinds and, in a special sector, by 'mixed marriage' groups, has brought out the fact that communion in prayer, meditation on the Bible, the liturgy of the Word, service, and social commitment bring irresistibly in their train the aspiration towards a joint celebration of the eucharist, which latter, however, cannot be real or form part of the current of ecumenism unless it is accompanied by active thinking about the mystery of the eucharist and unless it finds a recognized place in the life of our respective Churches. Theologians, engaged simultaneously in their research on dogma and their pastoral ministry among such groups, could not fail to respond to the appeal. From 1967 onwards, above all, that appeal was constantly in the background at Les Dombes, stimulating the endeavours of the Group and making them bear fruit that in turn stimulated and fed the thinking of many ecumenical groups.

Those endeavours are, of course, not at an end. While the joint celebration of the eucharist is the most significant step on the road to the unity of the Churches, it calls for an agreement about the respective ministries that rests at the same time on a doctrine as to their significance and the fact of their reconciliation. The 1968 and 1969 theses have already pointed the way; at its 1973 session the Group will begin to work out such an agreement.

Meanwhile, the fact of receiving a member of another Church at the communion table can, in circumstances to be defined from the pastoral angle, mark a stage on the road to unity. Thanks to the agreement we have arrived at, it can be said that among Christians who share communion in the body and blood of our Lord no shadow of ambiguity is cast on the faith which is theirs.

And so it was with gratitude that we welcomed the following declaration by the Joint Committee of the Catholic Church and the Lutheran and Reformed Churches in France, to which our doctrinal agreement on the eucharist had been presented:

> The Joint Committee regard [this text] as most important at a time when the question of 'eucharistic hospitality' is coming more and more to the fore.
>
> The Churches have instructed the Joint Committee to resume the study of the problem of a common eucharist. The Committee recommend that they examine this text closely and also draw their attention to its value to all Christian people for their better understanding of the real meaning of the eucharist.

The Ecumenical Movement has shed light on the certainty that 'the closer we come to Jesus Christ the closer we come to one another'. By penetrating together by faith into the mystery of the eucharist we are uniting ourselves more nearly to Jesus Christ and advancing towards our unity in him. It is in this hope that the Group of Les Dombes offers to the public the fruit of its labours.

SIGNATORIES OF THE AGREEMENT

ROMAN CATHOLIC
Paul Aymard, OSB
Joseph de Baciocchi, SM
René Beaupère, OP
Edmond Chavaz
Marc Clément
Robert Clément, SJ
Jacques Desseaux
André Fabre
Claude Gerest, OP
René Girault
Etienne Goutagny, OCR
Maurice Jourjon
Marie Leblanc, OSB
Pierre Michalon, PSS
André Perroux
Jean Roche, SJ
Bernard Sesboué, SJ
Maurice Villain, SM

PROTESTANT
Georges Appia
Claude Asmussen
Georges Besse
Henry Bruston
Edouard Diserens
Maurice Ferrier-Welti
Jean-Claude Ill
Michel Leplay
Louis Lévrier
Marc Lods
Hébert Roux
Brother Max Thurian, of Taizé
André Veimert
Gaston Westphal

NOTES

References to pages in this book are in brackets, thus [ ].

1. M. Villain, *L'Abbé Paul Couturier, apotre de l'Unite chrétienne* (Tournai 1957) especially pp. 140-77; R. Beaupère, M. Villain, J. de Baciocchi, H. Bruston, G. Martelet, in *Verbum Caro* 70 and *Dialogue oecuménique* (Taizé 1964); J. de Baciocchi, 'Fidélite dogmatique et recherche oecuménique' in *Foi et Vie* (*Hommage à Jean Bosc*) (April—September 1971), pp. 14-21
   The 'theses' of Les Dombes have been published as follows:
   (i) Those of the years 1956 to 1962 ii *Verbum Caro 70* and *Dialogue oecuménique,* (Taizé 1964) (commentaries: J. de Baciocchi, H. Bruston, and G. Martelet) and in *Unité Chrétienne,* pages documentaires No. 9, February 1968 (commentary: J. de Baciocchi)
   (ii) Those of the years 1965 to 1969 in *Foi et Vie,* loc. cit. (commentary J. de Baciocchi) and in *Unité Chrétienne,* pages documentaires No. 23 (July 1971)
2. This does not mean that Christ is localized in the bread and wine or that these latter undergo any physico-chemical change. Cf. St Thomas, ST III. 76, 3-5; III. 77, 5-8; Calvin, *Christ. Inst.* I, 11.13; IV. 14.18
3. Certain Eastern Churches (e.g., the Copts) do not reserve the eucharist.

4. *Eucharisticum mysterium* (25 May 1967) Nos. 49 and 50
5. Cf. *La Cène du Seigneur,* a text adopted by the French Lutheran and Reformed Churches
6. Cf. Thesis No. 2 (1968)
7. These Christians are not thereby relieved of the obligation to consider whether their request is a legitimate one, having regard to the justice of their motives and the discipline of their own Church.
8. Some of these we mention for information:
   'Accord oecuménique sur l'eucharistie', in *Verbum Caro* No. 87 (1968), pp. 1-10
   'Lutherans and Catholics in the United States', in *Lutherans and Catholics in Dialogue* (1968), ch. III, The Eucharist as Sacrifice [pp. 33-49]
   Agreement between the Lutheran and Reformed Churches in France (*La Cène du Seigneur*) in *Information—Evangélisation* No. 1 (1971), p. 46
   Document on the ecumenical dialogue of the joint Roman Catholic–WCC Working Party, in *Information Service* (1967/3)
   Maurice Villain, SM, 'Peut-il y avoir succession apostolique en dehors de la chaine de l'imposition de mains?', in in *Concilium* 34 (April 1968)
   Jérôme Hamer, OP, 'Etapes sur le chemin de l'Unité; le problème de l'intercommunion', in *Documentation catholique* (1968)
   Adrian Hastings, 'Intercommunion', in *One in Christ* (1971/2)
   J. Moingt, SJ, 'Problèmes d'intercommunion', in *Etudes* (February 1970)
   ARCIC: *Agreed Statement,* (1971) [pp. 23-31]
   The following may also be consulted: V. Vajta, *Intercommunion avec Rome?* (Paris 1970)
   L'Eucharistie and *Vers l'Intercommunion,* Coll. 'Eglises en dialogue' (Paris 1971), and the dossiers published in *Lumière et Vie* and *Foi et Vie* (Ecumenical Group of Aix-en-Provence 1967) and *Istina* (1970-71)
9. Cf. Theses No. 2 (1967)
10. This was the subject of the Group's study at the 1972 session at Les Dombes; see *Pour une réconciliation des ministères* (Taizé 1972)
11. This agreement should lead our Churches which recognize in one another a real ecclesial standing (cf. in particular the Decree *Unitatis Redintegratio,* sections 3 and 19) to declare by means of an act of reconciliation the existence in the body of each a real apostolic ministry. Such an act, whose specific conditions would remain to be defined, would enable members of each of our Churches to recognize in the minister presiding over the eucharist of the other Church the authentic representative of Christ among them.

THE
EUCHARIST IN
ECUMENICAL
THOUGHT

Statement of the
Faith and Order Commission
of the
World Council of Churches

LOUVAIN 1971

THE EUCHARIST
IN ECUMENICAL THOUGHT

The Faith and Order Commission meeting at Bristol, England, in August 1967, adopted the report of the section on 'The Holy Eucharist', and accepted the following recommendation:

> That there be drawn up a résumé of the emerging ecumenical consensus on the eucharist, drawing on the work of Lund, Montreal, Aarhus, and Bristol, and on the work of regional groups and of individual scholars related to the ecumenical discussions of the eucharist. On the basis of this résumé the draft of a popular booklet, perhaps with illustrations, should be prepared under the direction of the Secretariat. Booklets could then be printed separately in the language and idiom of the various countries, in consultation with representatives of National Councils of Churches and with experts in communication. In this way a wider public could be informed about ecumenical liturgical developments.

The 'Résumé of the Emerging Ecumenical Consensus on the Eucharist' which follows is based on paragraphs produced by the Third and Fourth World Conferences on Faith and Order, at Lund in 1952 and Montreal in 1963, and by the Faith and Order Commission itself at Bristol in 1967, being drawn from the official records of these meetings.

The two World Conferences, and the Commission itself, were composed of scholars and churchmen, both lay and clerical, appointed or approved by the Churches as their official representatives for Faith and Order work. The substance of the paragraphs was produced by sections of these conferences, or of the Commission, which were broadly representative of the major confessional families. In every case the section, in turn, had drawn upon the work of a theological or study commission that had laboured over several years, and upon the work of specialists in the field.

While the representatives of the Churches, and the methods employed in each section or group differed because of personalities and circumstances, the results of their labours have an official character which cannot be attributed to the writings of individuals or of other less representative groups, due to the fact that the section reports were in each case submitted for criticism and amendment to a plenary assembly widely representative of the Churches. It should be recognized that this résumé represents a stage in a process and will probably be superseded by further ecumenical consensus arrived at by a similar process. It will be continually subject to clarification, improvement and extension in the ongoing work for Christian unity.

While we cannot be fully content with the consensus represented in this statement we believe that it reflects a degree of agreement that could not have been foreseen even five years ago, and that our future is bright with hope.

PREAMBLE

'Baptism, once performed and never repeated, leads us into the continuous worshipping life of the royal priesthood, the people of God. In the eucharist or Lord's supper constantly repeated and always including both word and sacrament we proclaim and celebrate a memorial of the saving acts of God. What God did in the incarnation, life, death, resurrection, and ascension of Christ, he does not do again; the events are unique; they cannot be repeated or extended. . . .'[1] 'Christ himself, with all he has accomplished for us and for all creation . . . is present' in the eucharist.[2]

The eucharist is essentially a single whole, consisting usually of the following elements in varying sequence:

proclamation of the Word of God, in different ways;
intercession for the whole Church and the world;
thanksgiving for creation and redemption;
the words of Christ's institution of the sacrament;
prayer for the gift of the Holy Spirit;

prayer for the Lord's coming and for the manifestation of
  his Kingdom;
the Lord's prayer;
the breaking of the bread;
the eating and drinking in communion with Christ and each
  member of the Church.[3]

This list of liturgical items is not meant to exclude reference
to others, such as 'the expression of contrition, the declaration
of forgiveness of sins, the affirmation of faith in credal form, the
celebration of the communion of saints . . . and the self-dedica-
tion of the faithful to God. We assume that the person who presides will be someone recognized by his church as authorized to
do so.[4]

The eucharist contains a great richness and variety of meaning. Individuals as well as ecclesiastical traditions hold (widely)
varying views. No document could be a complete exposition of
every aspect of eucharistic thought. Moreover any attempt to
expound the eucharist is bound to deal separately with different
aspects, whereas the eucharist is essentially a single whole. But
this paper reflects the extent to which there is now a wide and
growing agreement on many of the aspects of eucharistic thought.

1 THE EUCHARIST: THE LORD'S SUPPER

The eucharist is the sacramental meal, the new paschal meal of
the people of God, which Christ, having loved his disciples until
the end, gave to them before his death, shared with them after
his resurrection and commanded them to hold until his return.

This meal of bread and wine is the sacrament, the effective
sign and assurance of the presence of Christ himself, who sacrificed his life for all men and who gives himself to them as the
bread of life; because of this, the eucharistic meal is the sacrament of the body and blood of Christ, the sacrament of his real
presence.[5]

In the eucharist the promise of the presence of the crucified
and risen Christ is fulfilled in a unique way for the faithful, who
are sanctified and unified in him, reconciled in love to be his
servants of reconciliation in the world.

2 THE EUCHARIST: THANKSGIVING TO THE FATHER

The eucharist is the great thanksgiving to the Father for everything which he accomplished in creation and redemption, for everything which he accomplishes now in the Church and in the world in spite of the sins of men, for everything that he will accomplish in bringing his kingdom to fulfilment. Thus the eucharist is the benediction (*berakah*) by which the Church expresses its thankfulness to God for all his benefits.[6]

The eucharist is the great sacrifice of praise by which the Church speaks on behalf of the whole creation. 'For the world which God has reconciled to himself is present at every eucharist: in the bread and wine, in the persons of the faithful, and in the prayers they offer for themselves and for all men. As the faithful and their prayers are united in the Person of our Lord and to his intercession they are transfigured and accepted. Thus the eucharist reveals to the world what it must become.'[7]

3 THE EUCHARIST: MEMORIAL (ANAMNESIS) OF CHRIST

'Christ instituted the eucharist, sacrament of his body and blood with its focus upon the cross and resurrection, as the *anamnesis* of the whole of God's reconciling action in him. Christ himself with all he has accomplished for us and for all creation (in his incarnation, servanthood, ministry, teaching, suffering, sacrifice, resurrection, ascension, and Pentecost) is present in this *anamnesis* as is also the foretaste of his Parousia and the fulfilment of the Kingdom. The *anamnesis* in which Christ acts through the joyful celebration of his Church thus includes this representation and anticipation. It is not only a calling to mind of what is past, or of its significance. It is the Church's effective proclamation of God's mighty acts. By this communion with Christ the Church participates in that reality.

'Anamnetic representation and anticipation are realized in thanksgiving and intercession. The Church proclaiming before God the mighty acts of redemption in thanksgiving, beseeches him to give the benefits of these acts to every man. In thanksgiving and intercession, the Church is united with the Son, its great High Priest and Intercessor.

'The *anamnesis* of Christ is the basis and source of all Christian prayer. So our prayer relies upon and is united with the continual intercession of the risen Lord. In the eucharist, Christ empowers us to live with and to pray with him as justified sinners joyfully and freely fulfilling his will.'[8]

'With contrite hearts we offer ourselves as a living and holy sacrifice, a sacrifice which must be expressed in the whole of our daily lives. Thus united to our Lord, and to the Church triumphant, and in fellowship with the whole Church on earth, we are renewed in the covenant sealed by the blood of Christ.'[9]

'Since the *anamnesis* of Christ is the very essence of the preached Word as it is of the eucharist, each reinforces the other. Eucharist should not be celebrated without the ministry of the Word, and the ministry of the Word points to, and is consummated in the eucharist.'[10]

4 THE EUCHARIST: GIFT OF THE SPIRIT

'The anamnesis leads to *epiklesis,* for Christ in his heavenly intercession prays the Father to send the Spirit upon his children. For this reason, the Church, being under the New Covenant, confidently prays for the Spirit, in order that it may be sanctified and renewed, led into all truth and enpowered to fulfil its mission in the world. *Anamnesis* and *epiklesis* . . . cannot be conceived apart from communion. Moreover it is the Spirit who, in our eucharist, makes Christ really present and given to us in the bread and wine, according to the words of institution.[1]

The gift of the Holy Spirit in the eucharist is a foretaste of the Kingdom of God: the Church receives the life of the new creation and the assurance of the Lord's return (*maranatha*).

'We agree that the whole action of the eucharist has an epikletic character, i.e., that it depends upon the work of the Holy Spirit; we agree also that this aspect of the eucharist should find expression in the words of the liturgy. Some desire an invocation of the Holy Spirit upon the people of God and upon the whole eucharistic action, including the elements: some hold that the reference to the Spirit may be made in other ways.'[12]

'The consecration cannot be limited to a particular moment in the liturgy. Nor is the location of the epiklesis in relation to the words of institution of decisive importance. In the early liturgies the "prayer action" was thought of as bringing about the reality promised by Christ. A recovery of such an understanding may help to overcome our differences concerning a special moment of consecration.'[13]

5 THE EUCHARIST, COMMUNION OF THE BODY OF CHRIST

The eucharistic communion with Christ present, who nourishes the life of the Church, is at the same time communion with the body of Christ which is the Church. 'The sharing of the common loaf and the common cup in a given place demonstrates the oneness of the sharers with the whole Christ and with their fellow sharers in all times and places. By sharing the common loaf they show their unity with the Church catholic, the mystery of redemption is set forth, and the whole body grows in grace.'[14]

Because of its catholicity the eucharist is a radical challenge to the tendencies toward estrangement, separation, and fragmentation. Lack of local unity in church or society constitutes a challenge to the Christians in that place. A mockery is made of the eucharist when the walls of separation destroyed by Christ on his cross are allowed to reappear in church life—those between races, nationalities, tongues, and classes[15].

According to the promise of Christ, each faithful member of the body of Christ receives in the eucharist remission of sins and everlasting life, and is nourished in faith, hope and love.

Solidarity in the eucharistic communion of the body of Christ (*agape*) and responsible concern of Christians for one another and the world should be given specific expression in the liturgies, for example, 'in the mutual forgiveness of sins; the kiss of peace; the bringing of gifts for the communal meal and for distribution to the poor brethren; the specific prayer for the needy and suffering; the taking of the eucharist to the sick and those in prison. In this agapeic realization of eucharistic fullness, the ministry of deacons and deaconesses was (in the early Church) especially responsible. The place of such a ministry between the table and the needy properly testifies to the redeeming presence of Christ in the world. All these agapeic features of the eucharist are directly related to Christ's own testimony as a Servant, in whose servanthood Christians themselves participate by virtue of their union with him. As God in Christ has entered into the human situation, so should eucharistic liturgy be near to the concrete and particular situations of men.'[16]

6 THE EUCHARIST: MISSION TO THE WORLD

Mission is not simply a consequence of the eucharist. Whenever the Church is the Church, mission must be part of its life. At the eucharist the Church is supremely itself and is united with Christ in his mission.

The word is already present in the thanksgiving to the Father, where the Church speaks on behalf of the whole creation; in the memorial of Christ, where the Church united with its great High Priest and Intercessor prays for the world, in the prayer for the gift of the Holy Spirit, where the Church asks for sanctification and new creation.

Reconciled in the eucharist, the members of the body of Christ are servants of reconciliation amongst men and witnesses of the joy of resurrection. Their very presence in the world implies full solidarity with the sufferings and hopes of all men, to whom they can be signs of the love of Christ who sacrificed himself on the cross and gives himself in the eucharist.

The eucharist is also the feast of the continuing apostolic harvest, where the Church rejoices for the gifts received in the world and welcomes every man of good will.

7 THE EUCHARIST: END OF DIVISIONS

'When local churches, no matter how humble, share in the eucharist they experience the wholeness of the Church and reveal it in its fullness—its members, its faith, its history, and its special gifts. Eucharistic celebrations, therefore, are always concerned with the whole Church and the Church is concerned with every eucharistic celebration. Since the earliest days baptism has been understood as the sacrament by which believers are incorporated into the body of Christ and are endowed by the Holy Spirit. When, therefore, the right of baptized believers and their ministers to participate in and preside over eucharistic celebrations in one Church is called in question by those who preside over and are members of other eucharistic congregations, the catholicity of the eucharist is obscured. On the other hand, in so far as a Church claims to be a manifestation of the whole Church, it should recognize that the whole Church is involved in its pastoral and administrative regulations.'[17]

'The question of intercommunion demands above all an inquiry about the nature, as well as the necessity, of the ministry in general, and of episcopacy in particular. The Churches should be urged to undertake a positive re-assessment of the ministry, both as it is manifested in their own order and in that of other Churches. In particular, they should address themselves to the following questions:

a The 'Catholic' Churches should ask whether the ministries of non-episcopal Churches—quite apart from their possession of apostolic succession or their lack of it—do not in fact contain elements of value (such as charismatic or extraordinary ministries), and if so of what value such elements may be.

b The 'Protestant' Churches, on the other hand, should reconsider, in the light of the ecumenical movement, the value of the commonly accepted ministry of the early Church and of pre-Reformation times.

c 'Protestant' as well as 'Catholic' Churches should further ask themselves whether, in spite of the widely divergent appearance of pre-Reformation and Reformation ministries, a measure of hidden identity may not in fact have been preserved. Does the fact that the Reformers rejected the name or title of a given ecclesiastical order necessarily prove that the reality behind the name was also rejected? Or again, does the fact that a name or title has been preserved, by itself, constitute a proof that the intended reality has been retained? In what cases is the rejection of episcopacy or of priests absolute and final? In what cases does the apparent rejection of the old ecclesiastical orders mean only the rejection of certain sociological forms and modalities? How far are they susceptible to the principle of 'economy'?"[18]

The best way towards unity in eucharistic celebration and communion is the renewal itself of the eucharist in the different

Churches, in regard to teaching and liturgy. As the eucharist is the new liturgical service Christ has given to the Church, it seems normal that it should be celebrated not less frequently than every Sunday, or once a week. As the eucharist is the new sacramental meal of the people of God, it seems also normal that every faithful should receive communion at every celebration.

'As the Churches in their eucharistic experience move toward the fullness which is in Christ, the problem of intercommunion will move toward its solution.'[19]

NOTES

1. Montreal, No. 116
2. Bristol, II 1
3. See Montreal, No. 118
4. Montreal, No. 118
5. See Lund, p. 54, b
6. Montreal, No. 118, b II
7. Bristol, III 2
8. Bristol, II 1-3; see Lund, p. 54, a-c, and Montreal, No. 117
9. Montreal, No. 117
10. Bristol, II 5 a
11. Bristol, II 4
12. Bristol, Appendix 4
13. Bristol, II 5 c
14. Bristol, III 1
15. See Bristol, III 4
16. Bristol, IV 4
17. Bristol, III 3
18. Bristol, V 2
19. Bristol V